Columbia Sportswear Company's

GROUSE
of NORTH AMERICA
A Cross-Continental Hunting Guide

By Tom Huggler

Willow Creek Press
An Imprint of NorthWord Press, Inc.
Box 1360, Minocqua, WI 54548

For all the dogs who could not go, especially Lady Macbeth.

Grouse of North America: a cross-continental hunting guide / by
Tom Huggler.
    p.   cm.
ISBN 1-55971-074-80
1. Grouse shooting.   2. Grouse shooting--North America.
SK325.G7H84   1990
799.2'48616--dc20   90-45222
                                            CIP

Copyright © 1990 by Tom Huggler

Published September, 1990 by:
Willow Creek Press
An Imprint of NorthWord Press, Inc.
Box 1360
Minocqua, WI 54548
(715) 356-9800

For a free catalog describing NorthWord's line
of nature books and gifts, call 1-800-336-5666.

Designed by Origins Design, Inc.
Cover design by Mary Shafer

A limited edition of 4,000 copies, entitled
Columbia Sportswear's *Grouse of North America*,
has been numbered and signed by the author.
Ordering information is available from:

COLUMBIA SPORTSWEAR COMPANY
P.O. Box 83239
Portland, OR 97283-0239
1-800-547-8066

Printed in U.S.A.

ISBN 1-55971-074-8

Many people played behind-the-scenes but important roles in the process that has culminated with this book. Some of them showed me places to go hunting, a few journeyed with me for short periods, and others put me up and fed me and my dogs.

I want to thank Dave and Myra Wickham (Nebraska); Larry Johnson and Dick Dixon (Colorado); Chris Madson (Wyoming); Steve Shimek, Jeff Herbert, Roy Olsen, Mark Lewis and Mike Stevens (Montana); Ray Heupel, Terry and Linda Strand, Jim and Norma Fuglie, Terry Harzinski, Denny and Cathy Mills and Byron and Tolly Holtan (North Dakota); Gordon Gullion and Dan and Kim Nelson (Minnesota); Tom and Patti Petrie (Wisconsin); Mike Pearce, Mike Smyth, Jeff Graves, Lawrence and Ruth Smith, Mike Murphy, Jim Reid, Thayne Smith and Bill and Joan Harmon (Kansas); John Long, Randy Collins, Mark Guilford, Bill Hollister and Carl Parker (New York); Tim Leary, Doug Truax and Jamie Dickinson (Vermont); John Lanier and Tim Jones (New Hampshire); and many Michigan friends, several of whom hunt with me in the upper peninsula each October.

Gerry Bethge of *Outdoor Life* magazine lent an editor's ears and my wife, Laura, offered a skilled pen for the initial editing. I appreciated their help as well as that of editors Tom and Chuck Petrie and Mary Shafer at NorthWord Press.

A dozen photographers contributed images to supplement my own. I'm indebted to Ron Spomer, Tim Leary, Gary Zahm, Henry Zeman, Richard Smith, Dave Books, Michael Francis, Randy Carrels, Tom Martinson, Dale Spartas and Karl, Steve and Dave Maslowski.

I wish to thank Steve Tracey and Ron Barger of the Starcraft Corporation for the loan of a motorhome and for gracing our Michigan grouse hunting camp with memorable recipes and good companionship.

A very special thank you goes to the Columbia Sportswear Company, without whose sole sponsorship the journey and this book would not have been possible. Bart Bonime and Tim Boyle believed in this project from the day we discussed it in November, 1988, while chukar hunting on a rain-slick hill in Oregon. And Mary Marckx supplied me with wonderful Columbia Sportswear garments that kept me warm and dry and added immeasurably to my comfort.

This Georgia hunter moves into a grouse point by his English pointer. (Photograph - Tom Huggler)

"We are here on the planet only once,
and we might as well get a feel for the place."

—Annie Dillard

In the fall of 1989, I made three trips across America in a motorhome. During those three months and 11,000 miles, I wanted to find, study, photograph, hunt, kill, eat and get mounted the several species of native grouse that inhabit North America. And I wanted to write this book.

I learned many things, perhaps the most important of which is that to love grouse is to love the special places where grouse live. Places like the shores of Lake Sakakawea in North Dakota, where the soft brown hills were woven with purple asters, reminding me of slopes of heather on the Scottish Highlands, only there were sharptails, and not red grouse, in North Dakota. The red grouse of Europe is the same bird, or nearly so, that we North Americans call the willow ptarmigan, a grouse that lives in tundra of the arctic. I found his cousin, the white-tailed ptarmigan, at 13,000 feet on a September day in Colorado when the white mountain peaks pierced a lapis sky in sharp relief, and cottonwood fuzz, levitated by thermals, drifted across the saddle where my dogs and I walked.

A special place, indeed, and well worth the painful climb.

Later, I camped in the immense Shirley Basin north of Medicine Bow, Wyoming, and ate fried sage grouse under a canopy fired by millions of tiny lights, not one of which was artificial. In Montana, another hunter, a golden eagle, searched for blue grouse above a talus of broken shale that clattered like plateware when I stumbled across it. In Kansas, the lesser prairie chickens arrived on crooked wings above penumbral hills before the sun could soak them in orange light.

There were special places for ruffed grouse, too, in Wisconsin, my native Michigan, New York, Vermont and New Hampshire where the birds tunneled into snowdrifts to survive

His journey took him to many of the beautiful places where grouse live. (Photograph - Tom Huggler)

a night of 20 below zero and then shocked us with explosive flight the next day.

As a writer, you know you have to go when you have depleted your experiences and are using the same words and describing the same scenes over and over. It had been four years since I had traveled a long way, alone, for birds. Then, the subject was quail; those three months of journeying in 1985 I still consider one of those clear and definitive periods of life from which we date things of lesser significance. It was obvious that the time had come to take to the road again.

You realize the necessity of going at the moment that you become properly suspended in the journey itself. That occurs only when the cord connecting you to family and home stretches the other way as well—to a motorhome, the dogs in tow, the people you just told goodbye, the ones you will meet tomorrow—and pulls you forward as powerfully as back. When that happens, the writer can write accurately, which is to say, truthfully.

Precipitating my travels for grouse were a marriage, a honeymoon in France, and a move to a new city, all of which left me temporarily confused.

Going on the road put these changes into perspective. The thin mountain air and a few $1.25 margaritas at two-mile-high Leadville, Colorado, helped. Dave Wickham and I were attempting to remove the taste of a nearly inedible chicken dinner at the Golden Rose Restaurant and Bar after taking an armed walk up a mountainside to look for a ptarmigan that was not home. I had met Wickham, who trains bird dogs in Nebraska and has a Denver cousin who knows something about ptarmigan, in the Holiday Inn bar in Ogalalla a couple of years earlier. I have this habit of saving telephone numbers written on matchbook covers.

Anyway, Dave slid his business card among the many others lying underneath the thick glass that covered our table. "Don't you have a card?" he wondered. I didn't. So I borrowed one of his and wrote, "Have Bird Dogs. Will travel." Then I added my new address.

Rays from a sun about to drop below a mountain peak streamed through the restaurant window and fired several pieces of stained glass into fantastic reds, greens and yellows. My friend, who has hunted sharptails and prairie chickens in the Sand Hills, licked the salt from the edge of a fresh drink and said, "I love to hunt pheasants and I dearly love to hunt quail, but there is something about grouse that's special. I can't explain it."

I don't know if I can either. But I will try.

Taking field notes in Kansas. (Photograph - Ron Spomer)

I killed grouse because the alternative was to look at photos, not birds in the hand, and to cook hamburgers for dinner and to run my dogs on game-farm pheasants. That is only part of the truth. The rest lies in the thrill of being a predator, but a predator with a conscience. Deciding when and when not to kill involves a complicated set of variables: sporting chance, laws such as bag limits, local scarcity and abundance even when the law permits killing, and the likelihood of a clean kill versus a certain cripple. The little 28 gauge gun I used to collect the grouse species was self-limiting in this respect.

I hunted because hunting made me an active participant in nature. The hunter not only sharpens his power of observation, but, more importantly, he increases his understanding of the game he seeks and begins to see the interrelationships of things, living and non-living, that contribute to its environment.

I have heard it said that the photographer and the bird watcher are hunters, too, but it is different for them. They are voyeurs, not hunters. Because they do not hold a warm, lifeless bird in the hand, they cannot experience the bittersweetness of triumph and sorrow that is so uniquely human. And so their pain or their outrage over the loss of a species or its habitat—usually one and the same—is always secondary. It is sympathetic but not empathetic, and that is why many of the spectators of blood sport cannot separate feeling from fact.

Each of us, hunter and nonhunter, contributes carbon monoxide and fluorocarbons to the atmosphere. Our bodies decompose inside vaults of indestructable marble or concrete. Our ashes remain from the final and ultimate pollution of the very air we breathe. In the end, what do we give back to the earth that nourished us?

As participants in nature, we can at least contribute an understanding and a reverence and, to a degree, a protection of sorts. Today's hunter is a conservationist, even though nothing in history or religion or literature has prepared him for conservation. The ancient Greeks knew nothing of it, nor did any of the other great civilizations, except the Orientals. God may have given man dominion over the earth, but he did not tell him how to conserve the earth's resources, finite or renewable.

Necessity is the mother of invention, and conservation, which in its strictest interpretation—that is, stripped of value—is a numbers phenomenon. Only we, in our modern judgment and wisdom, can decide what to save or not save, what to manage and what to destroy. I'd like those decisions to be made by men who carry guns or, at the very least, who respect those of us that do.

The author holds a lesser prairie chicken in Kansas. (Photograph - Ron Spomer)

My trips across America to hunt grouse changed me because I saw and began to understand the connections, not just between the birds and the places where they live but also between the living and nonliving objects within those places.

I wondered about a drop of rain in Kansas and how it impacts seed growth in a head of indiangrass. And how that seed, fully matured, scatters from the wing of a meadowlark, falls to ground, catches between a toenail of my Brittany, and is removed that night by me 200 miles away at a rest stop in eastern Nebraska. Does its journey end there, an infertile seed, or will it drop between pavement cracks and sprout? Or will the seed imbed itself in the tread of an Atlas Global van and hitchhike to Colorado?

We all journey. We all interconnect. Beyond the sore muscles and the parade of gasoline pit stops is the other journey, the one that begins with a dream and ends with an experience. Thoreau was right: "Our horizon is never quite at our elbows." And so I suppose a man could spend his time more foolishly than driving throughout the country in search of grouse.

This book is a dialogue of what I learned from reading about grouse, from interviewing people who care about grouse, and from walking in the places where grouse live.

Whether you come along vicariously, through the photos and descriptions in this book, or set out on your own odyssey, I hope your journey, too, is replete with peace and wonder.

Tom Huggler
Lansing, Michigan

Grouse eat more than 100 kinds of fruit and plant material. These are frozen highbush cranberries. (Photograph - Tom Huggler)

"What is man without other beasts? If all the beasts were gone, man would die from a loneliness of spirit. Whatever happens to the beasts will soon happen to man."

—Chief Seattle

The Family of Grouse

Say "grouse" and most hunters think of ruffed grouse, the king of the upland gamebirds. They seek ruffed grouse throughout Canada, in southern portions of Alaska, and in most of the lower 48 states. Ruffed grouse are native to 39 states and have been introduced to three others: Colorado, Oklahoma and Nevada. The only states without these noble birds are Arizona, New Mexico, Texas, Louisiana, Mississippi and Florida. The kill in the Upper Great Lakes region, where ruffs are most abundant, varies between one-half million and one and one-quarter million birds each year for Minnesota, Wisconsin, Michigan and Ontario.

At least six other species of grouse, all of which are plentiful enough to warrant hunting, also inhabit North America. They include the sharptail, prairie chicken, sage grouse, blue grouse, spruce grouse and ptarmigan. In his book *Grouse of the World*, University of Nebraska researcher Paul Johnsgard lists the three races of ptarmigan (rock, willow and white-tailed) as separate species, thus bringing the number to nine. Other scientists count the lesser prairie chicken as a separate species, which adds one more. Including the extinct heath hen makes a total of eight to 11 species of grouse that lived on the continent at one time.

Sharptails follow ruffed grouse in popularity as a game species with hunters killing upwards of 700,000 each year. Blue and spruce grouse each annually contribute about a half-million individuals to hunters' game bags. Biologists estimate that about 300,000 ptarmigan are taken each year, many for subsistence by native hunters in the Far North. The annual bag of prairie chickens is 50,000 to 75,000.

Ruffed grouse are capable of making slim targets of themselves, both in trees and in flight. (Photograph - Tom Martinson)

A Grouse for Every Habitat

A discovery that fascinated me during my travels was learning that a grouse type occupies nearly every major habitat the land offers. Ptarmigan, for example, live above treeline in high altitudes and in tundra of both the high and low arctic where they feed on stunted willow and low-growing shrubs. Sage grouse require sagebrush grasslands of the semi-arid West. Prairie chickens choose open grasslands, and sharptails select shorter prairie fringed with brush. Ruffed grouse want taller cover—boskets of aspen and other hardwoods mixed with conifers. Blue grouse, on the other hand, seek the forest edge of conifers sprinkled with hardwoods, and spruce grouse demand dense coniferous forests.

Of further intrigue is how grouse use available cover in terms of its vegetative height. Thus, from lichen-covered stones in inch-high tundra to 120-foot tall Douglas fir, there are few places in North America that a grouse does not call home.

In some regions, the territories of individual species may overlap, and interbreeding and hybridization of young may occur. While visiting Alaska a few years ago, I was shocked to find a dead sharp-tailed grouse along the highway. Later, I learned they were fairly common in Alaska, along with ruffed, spruce and blue grouse and the three races of ptarmigan. I have since discovered that Alaska and northern Canada offer outstanding hunting opportunities for most species of grouse because the birds are usually in good supply and hunting pressure is almost nonexistent.

One place where a species of grouse once thrived but is now extinct is the coastal grasslands and scrub-oak barrens of the northeastern U.S. This was the home of the heath hen, the eastern race of the prairie chicken, until habitat destruction and relentless hunting—the same one-two punch that ruined the passenger pigeon—destroyed it. The last heath hen, an eight-year-old male, boomed for the final time on a fire-ravaged plain at Martha's Vineyard in March of 1932.

I would give anything to have seen just one.

The Evolution of Grouse

Some researchers believe that grouse, quail, pheasants, turkeys and jungle fowl evolved from a common ancestor, perhaps during the Cenozoic era 50 million years ago. Quail experienced their speciation and distribution in southern climates, and that is why in

Top left: This male sharptail, Columbian race, was photographed sitting in low sagebrush on a lek. (Photograph - Ron Spomer)
Top right: This male sage grouse was photographed in Montana. (Photograph - Dave Books)
Bottom: These Alaska willow ptarmigan were photographed feeding on willow leaves. (Photograph - Ron Spomer)

addition to six native types in the U.S. there are nine others in Mexico and Central America and 15 more in South America.

Because of its temperate climate, the central U.S. from east to west is home to both quail and grouse species. But grouse evolved along northerly latitudes. Their range is circumpolar in the northern hemisphere from about 26 degrees to 81 degrees latitude. According to Johnsgard, nine of the 16 global species are native to North America, a fact which lends some evidence to the continent as the evolutionary center.

Most New World grouse species have Old World counterparts. The hazel grouse of eastern Europe and China chooses the same type of habitat as our ruffed grouse. The Caucasian black grouse of northern Europe and Siberia lives in habitat favored by the willow ptarmigan. The black grouse is similar to our blue grouse, and the sharp-winged grouse of Russia lives in the same deep conifers as the spruce grouse and likely evolved from it—or vice versa. Only the capercaillie, the world's largest grouse at seven to eight pounds, lacks a New World clone.

On the other hand, there are no European or Asian grouse like our sharptails, prairie chickens and sage grouse. This seems unusual because of the vast Old World steppes and semi-desert scrub habitats where such plains grouse might have evolved.

Although little is known about the evolution of individual grouse species, a 25 million-year-old fossil indicates that at least one species, long since extinct, lived in North America. Fossils from the middle Miocene epoch of about 15 million years ago suggest a blueprint for prairie grouse development. The ptarmigans and forest grouse (blue, spruce and ruffed) as we know them apparently had developed by the Pliocene or at least the Pleistocene, but the fossil record is far from complete. Ruffed grouse were apparently well established during the Pleistocene because remains that are 25,000 years old have been unearthed in several states.

Grouse are galliforms in that they use three of their four toes for scratching and their beaks for pecking seeds and ripping buds and leaves from shrubs and trees. They resemble pheasants and partridges, but not all scientists agree as to their taxonomy. Johnsgard, who surveyed all the available literature through 1982, places the subfamily Tetraoninae—the grouse and ptarmigans—under the family Phasianidae—pheasantlike birds. *Bonasa* (Latin for bison, or bellowing bull) is the genera shared by ruffed and hazel grouse. The ptarmigans are termed *Lagopus* (Greek for hare-footed, referring to the feet covered with feathers). Prairie

All grouse grow membranous combs on their toes to help them walk in snow and to perch on branches while budding or roosting. (Photograph - Ron Spomer)
On following pages: Ruffed grouse tail feathers longer than six inches (the length of a dollar bill) usually belong to a male. Solid band across central tail feathers and two or more white dots on rump feathers are other indications. (Photograph - Tom Huggler)

chickens and sharptails comprise the genera *Tympanuchus* (In Greek, the word means echo of a drum). *Centrocercus* (the Greek derivative for spiny tail) applies only to the sage grouse. The capercaillies and black grouse are termed *Tetrao* (pheasant in Greek). *Dendragapus* (Greek for lover of trees) is the genera for spruce, blue and sharp-winged grouse.

How Grouse Are Different

Grouse differ from pheasants and partridges in that feathers cover their nostrils and grow over their legs, in some cases to the toes. Little comblike membranes that grow along the edges of the toes act as snowshoes and help budding and roosting grouse grip branches. The combs fall off in summer. Another difference: male grouse do not grow spurs on their legs as cock pheasants and some male partridges do.

All grouse have 10 primary wing feathers, 15 to 21 secondaries, and 14 to 22 tail feathers. Their large crops are capable of storing a huge amount of food for later digestion. They are ground nesters, and, except for the willow ptarmigan, the males do not participate in nest defense or brood rearing. Rather, they save their energy for advertising their sexual prowess over a period of several weeks each spring.

That is when male grouse "display" in ritualized dances to attract hens in order to breed them. Forest grouse display individually on the same drumming logs, rocks or tree branches their ancestors may have used for generations. Males of the other species display socially on breeding grounds called leks. The leks, which may also be used year after year, are typically found atop slopes where they can be seen for a long distance by females. The lek of the greater prairie chicken is called a booming ground; for the lesser species, it becomes a gobbling ground. Sage grouse display on a strutting ground, and sharptails dance on a dancing ground. Hens select their partners, which are nearly always one of a few dominant cocks that occupy primary positions on the lek.

The number of lek-displaying males may vary from as few as 10 to 70 or more among sage grouse. The males use a combination of visual attractants—inflating their balloonlike, colorful air sacs along the neck, and ritualized movements—and sounds such as vocal noises and stamping or drumming of the feet. Males also display briefly in the fall, presumably to teach young-of-the-year cocks the tricks of the trade.

Male grouse drum by capturing air between their wings while balanced on a drumming log. (Photograph - Maslowski)

The birds are exceptionally well adapted to their environments. The sage grouse is the only species that does not have a true gizzard because it has eaten the leaves of sagebrush for thousands of years and has no need to grind its food. The young of blue grouse are capable of flying at only six or seven days of age, and they may leave the hen before they are two weeks old. Ptarmigan turn white by degrees to correspond with their changing world as snow accumulates. Their plumage has higher insulating qualities than most other birds because when fluffed, the feathers are designed to trap more air. Willow ptarmigan are the only monogamous grouse, and the males are perfectly capable of raising hatched chicks to maturity in a hostile world. The intestines of spruce grouse grow longer in winter to help digest up to a quarter-pound of pine needles, which the birds may consume at a single winter feeding.

All grouse species use the same pattern of flying—a burst of wing strokes followed by a gliding period. When flushed, forest grouse fly a short distance, usually no more than 300 or 400 yards. However, plains grouse and ptarmigan may fly several miles before resting, and the breast meat is dark because of increased dependence on wing power.

Willow and rock ptarmigan are great migrators; in Siberia, willow ptarmigan have been known to travel more than 350 miles in winter. Sharptails range 20 or more miles, and prairie chickens and sage grouse may migrate up to 100 miles in fall and spring. A friend of mine once followed a flock of greater chickens in Kansas for nine miles, and they were already in the air when he first observed them.

Forest grouse may or may not wander long distances. Blue grouse are vertical migrators, moving to higher altitudes in fall and returning to lower elevations in spring. A banded blue grouse moved 31 miles. A ruffed grouse traveled 71 miles although the usual fall dispersal is five miles or less. Spruce grouse are more stay-at-home creatures, rarely moving beyond a few acres of their original turf.

The Role of Hunting

Annual survival rates for grouse range from only 30 percent for willow ptarmigan to about 65 percent for blue grouse. Forty to 47 percent of ruffed and sharp-tailed grouse and greater prairie chickens live to see their first birthdays. Banded individuals of most grouse species have lived to be seven to eight years old. The oldest ruffed grouse ever recorded in the wild was 11. A penned bird lived to be 17.

Hunting has little or no impact on the overall mortality rates of grouse although too much hunting pressure over too long a period can affect local populations. Researchers and game managers alike are continually trying to to learn more about grouse. This includes their special habitat and life needs, how to protect them when necessary, and how to manage them for the enjoyment of both hunters and nonhunters.

An incredible amount of research has already been done on grouse, and more is constantly being published. In 1947, an exhaustive study of New York State ruffed grouse by Gardiner Bump and other researchers added a tremendous amount to the information pool, which already totaled more than 400 studies. Hundreds more have been added since. A check with the U.S. Fish and Wildlife Reference Service indicated that of 22,000 mostly unpublished reports on fish and game, more than 1,000 are grouse specific. Included are nearly 300 references on ruffed grouse and 600 on plains grouse. About 30 new studies are begun each year.

Whether we hunt or not, the more we know about grouse, the more we will appreciate them and attempt to save the often fragile places where they live. If you visit certain small-town libraries along Cape Cod, you may find a pamphlet called "The Heath Hen's Journey to Extinction." Unless someone removed it, a single feather will be attached to the inside cover. Anyone owning keys to a bulldozer should study that feather. Anyone planning to hook a chemical spray to his farm tractor should read the book.

Iceland

Greenland

Alaska

Canada

Pacific Ocean

United States

Atlantic Ocean

Ruffed Grouse
(Approximate Range)

*"You will know the woods when you are still a long way off by virtue of
a fragrance you can never quite forget and never quite remember."*

—James Thurber

The Ruffed Grouse

It is a long time between Octobers. This morning, two aspen leaves that had caught in the windshield wipers of my motorhome trembled yellow when I started the engine. Looking through the rearview mirror, I could see the breath of my dogs, pressing their eager noses against the window wire of the trailer kennel. My friends and I are also anxious to begin hunting. We bounce along a Michigan upper peninsula two-track, passing through landscapes of autumnal fire as good as any Robert Abbett painting. In front of us, a pickup truck, containing other hunters, sends a vortex of red and yellow leaves into the air. The leaves gently drift back to the road.

Too long between Octobers. Too long between the smell of mink oil on old leather. Between empty shotshells rattling next to live ones in the jacket pocket. Between whistles and dog bells and wet setters. Between stray grouse feathers on truck floor mats.

Serious gunners of ruffed grouse know all about October and the two-pound bird whose thunderclap flush makes hunters twitch in their sleep. In October, during what I call the middle season, grouse are in transition, spreading out to new territories, and likely to be anywhere. Studies show that grouse introduced to proper habitat may occupy a 100-square-mile area within only four years. Now is when they strut across manicured lawns and crash into plate-glass windows in the phenomenon known as "crazy flight." A friend of mine once shot a grouse that was stuffed with fermented wild grapes. When the bird fell, it careened into my friend's chest, splattering his shirt with purple.

The season, too, is in advent. Last week a maple leaf blushed; today, embarrassment has spread to the whole tree. The earth is exhaling for the last time this year,

and the pageantry of color, brief though it is, almost hurts the eyes. There is no finer time to be in the woods. One October day about 15 years ago, I made an offer on a 135-acre farm for sale in northern Michigan. The clincher? I found a dozen grouse stuffing themselves on beechnuts of the back forty. My offer was not accepted but I was told to go back there and hunt anytime, and I did until new owners began locking the gate.

Perhaps Leopold said it best: "Everybody knows that the autumn landscape in the north woods is the land, plus a red maple, plus a ruffed grouse."

I never tire of looking at the lovely markings of ruffed grouse, both red-phase and gray-phase birds. The black ruff is as regal as a Tudor monarch's collar. The fan, when spread, is a kaleidoscope of color and the intricate patterns of brown-tipped breast feathers and white diamonds on a mahogany back dazzle the eye. The bird's cryptic coloration is the essence of late autumn itself with its gunsmoke blue-grays and rich browns.

Grouse Through the Hunting Season

In Michigan, we seek October grouse in poolstick-size aspen, especially along the compromise of more mature hardwoods. Besides grouse there, we find woodcock, sometimes in scandalous numbers. The reduction process that withers the bracken fern and strips bare the trees opens up the covers. Grouse become increasingly concerned about overhead protection from raptors, and that is why they begin moving into heavier cover. This shift from upland stands of ridge oak and aspen-covered swells to lowland habitats of stream-bottom brush and swamp edges is subtle, occurring over several weeks. Usually by November it is complete. Then, aspen/alder edges with an understory of hazelbrush are prime locations.

The eating habits of grouse change, too. Although they still want green matter in November, they feed more heavily on fruits and begin turning to buds and catkins.

In some states, the hunting seasons open in September. The forest during this early period is a lush hell, nearly impossible to negotiate. Finding family broods can be difficult; hitting birds on the wing is tougher still. The lack of frost encourages pesky mosquitoes to hang on. We hunt anyway, in the farm country of southern Michigan, targeting brushlands and open woods near weed and crop fields. The edge of meadows or fields containing goldenrod and abutting heavier cover becomes productive, as long as there is some protective canopy. Grouse crops yield green plant materials, such as strawberry leaves and clover.

This fall hunting scene was photographed in Wisconsin. (Photograph - Tom Huggler)

Young birds shot near this forest/field edge are also full of insects. We keep an eye out for sandy lanes that snake through alternating fields and woods. Oval depressions in sunny patches of sand are proof that grouse dusted themselves there.

In some places the hunting seasons run well into the new year. During this late season, surviving grouse—their screening covers gone—are so hair-trigger nervous that they flush or run at the crunch of a boot in snow. Now, grouse seek lowland conifers interspersed with aspen. Pines with branches sweeping the ground provide protection from cold winds and predators alike. Multiflora rose, hawthorns and greenbrier near heavy woods are good spots to hunt. So, too, are blowdowns. A December deer hunter I know once watched nine grouse exit single file from a blowdown underneath his tree stand.

Grouse are snow lovers. They instinctively roost in deep, fluffy snow, usually in open, mature timber near food sites. Sometimes they squat in snow (look for yellow-green droppings about a half-inch long), and other times they burrow completely under. During periods of extremely cold weather, grouse may spend up to 22 hours of each day in a snow roost. In the absence of snow, they roost in conifers or thick aspens.

Aspen flower buds that began developing in leaf axils over the summer now become increasingly available. Early one afternoon while bowhunting for deer, I watched a downed aspen below my tree stand suddenly begin to shake violently. In a moment, I could see why: a grouse was ripping away at buds as though this was his last meal. Researchers have determined that a hungry grouse can pick off nearly 50 buds per minute. In a quarter-hour, a gluttonous grouse may consume the equivalent of a 150-pound person eating 27 pounds of food.

The grouse who lingers over dessert may not get the chance to digest his meal. Another time, while bowhunting in December, I watched a grouse fly 200 yards from roosting cover in a small belt of Scotch pines to a pod of aspens bordering an alfalfa field. For three consecutive evenings, just before dark, this bird zipped to the dining table, gobbled down a quick meal, then hurried back to his roost. He did not show on the fourth evening. I imagine a hawk or owl killed him. Had food and security been closer together, the grouse might have lived to strut on a drumming log the following spring.

Top: The author hunted with Tim Leary and his setter Spiller in Vermont during a December cold snap.
(Photograph - Tom Huggler)
Bottom: Late season snow and sub-zero temperatures make grouse skittish when they are hunted, especially with dogs.
Number six shot and modified choke is the ideal match. (Photograph - Tom Huggler)
On following pages: A ruffed grouse dined here. (Photograph - Tim Leary)

Hunting the Food Sources

Collective research indicates that the opportunistic ruffed grouse eats just about anything, even cockleburs, burdock, poison ivy, deadly nightshade berries and toxic mountain laurel leaves. Although New York grouse preferred aspen buds and flowers, followed by clover leaves and hazelnut buds, crop contents of a large number of birds revealed 65 different plant families totaling 414 species. Virginia grouse from the Allegheny Mountains showed an equal preference for acorns, grapes and greenbrier fruit and leaves. In Ohio, greenbrier fruits and leaves and aspen were followed by dogwood, grape, sumac and beech buds. Grouse on Vancouver Island liked salal fruit; in Idaho, they chose sedge and then blueberries; in Washington State, they gobbled buttercup, followed by black cottonwood, gooseberries and blackberries.

The best way to find out what grouse are eating in your locale is to examine the crop of your first kill.

During cold snaps of the late season, grouse expend more energy to stay warm. Studies show that 80 percent of birds are up before sunrise and ready for breakfast. Ninety-eight percent are still feeding after sunset.

Grouse Covers

I love to hunt ruffed grouse throughout the fall, but the middle season period of October and November is my favorite. I am not alone. My friend Tim Leary sets aside the entire month to hunt as many of the 150 covers he has mapped in Vermont and New Hampshire as possible. Beginning in the northern region of both states, he follows the leaf drop south. "It's like visiting old friends each year," he explained, "knowing they have changed but hoping they have not changed too much."

There is a certain joy in finding and naming your own covers. You hope that no other grouse hunter ever goes there; it is possible to trick yourself into believing that no one does. That is why I pick up my shotshell hulls and grow disturbed when I find the spent shells of other hunters.

New Englanders are more secretive and more protective of their covers than are grouse hunters in the Great Lakes region, or anywhere else, for that matter. Most New England covers are depressingly small, capable of being hunted in a half-hour or so, and

Top left: Entrance to New Hampshire grouse cover in October. (Photograph - Tim Leary)
Top right: A scene from the author's hunting camp in Michigan's upper peninsula. (Photograph - Tom Huggler)
Bottom: The average grouse hunter shoots at least three shells for every bird in the bag. (Photograph - Tim Leary)

productive of only one or two birds per season. The covers rarely go by names that give away their location, as in The Ranville Road Cover. Rather, they are called names like the Washing Machine Cover, where a nearsighted hunter once mistook a discarded washing machine for a setter on point.

"We name our grouse," said Jamie Dickinson, an instructor in the Orvis Shooting School who hunts Manchester, Vermont-area covers on his lunch hour. "And we get to know them on a personal basis. We know where to expect their flush, right down to the apple tree."

In Vermont, no new covers are being made, and the ones left are in regression. In New Hampshire, I hunted with federal wildlife biologist John Lanier and writer Tim Jones in abandoned apple orchards tucked into hillsides of the White Mountains National Forest. The spruce and hardwood forest sprawls over 700,000 acres of northern New Hampshire. Lanier is the only management biologist. Thirty million people, some of them hunters, live within a day's drive of the forest.

When I got to New England it was December, and I was greeted with deep snow and frigid weather. October is the right time to go, but I was in the upper peninsula then, driving down that two-track and watching autumn swirl by the motorhome windows. Two days before I had seen my first fiery maple of the year in a friend's yard in Brainerd, Minnesota. For a month, I had been hunting the wide-open vistas of the West where a man can squint and see 40 miles. Today, I would plunge into broomstick aspen so thick I would not be able to see 40 yards.

It was the only time in my life I have felt claustrophobic while hunting grouse.

You know you are in the right cover, at least in the Upper Midwest, when unseen hands knock your cap to the ground and invisible fingers reach for your eyes and ears. By evening, the backs of your hands should be cat-scratched with fine white lines and maybe a drop or two of dried blood. Shooting birds in grouse cover like that requires a little skill and a lot of luck.

Grouse Guns and Hunting Tactics

The skill comes from experience. You learn to carry your gun at port arms while looking over the muzzle and using your forearms to push branches aside. I press the stock tightly to my ribs, much like a Sporting Clays shooter, for fast pullup; place my index finger

Top: Rewards of hunting grouse might be a bird, or a wild apple or two. (Photograph - Ron Spomer)
Bottom: Waves of farm abandonments have occurred at least three times in New England during the past century.
Abandoned farms make good grouse cover. (Photograph - Tim Leary) On following pages: Because of the cold weather and the fact that they
represent generations of selective breeding, English setters are the most popular dog for hunting ruffed grouse. (Photograph - Maslowski)

above the trigger guard on the same plane as the barrel; and keep my thumb on the safety. You learn to put your feet down solidly to avoid being off balance for any part of a second because that is typically when a grouse will choose to flush.

There are two kinds of grouse gunners. The spray-and-pray type fires as quickly as possible at the first sight of feathers. A barrel choked skeet or one chopped-down to riot-gun proportions, then loaded with number 8 or 9 shot, will bring down a fair number of early season grouse. The large number of small pellets will strain through the canopy of leaves and drop young birds not yet fully feathered. The method works because three of every four grouse that flush do so under 25 yards from the hunter.

The speed-and-lead shooter swings with the bird and then ahead of the bird until he spots an opening. Timed properly, grouse and shot charge meet in an explosion of feathers. An improved cylinder or modified barrel scattergun stoked with number $7 1/2$ size shot is the best choice, unless you are also gunning for woodcock. Then, load with 8s.

Before I knew better, I used to hunt grouse with a 12 gauge 870 Wingmaster pump and 30-inch full-choke barrel. Eventually I downsized to a Citori Superlight in 20 gauge. Today, I carry a 28 gauge over and under, a Classic Doubles remake of the Winchester 101. My reasons are self-limitation and curiosity. Depending on the circumstances of cover and bird behavior, I can be both a spray-and-pray and speed-and-lead shooter. I screw in chokes of skeet in the bottom barrel and IC in the upper tube and drop in $3/4$ oz. target loads of number 8 shot. That combination is good for early season grouse, and it is deadly on woodcock that jump above the standing bracken fern like stringed puppets.

Later in the season, when the canopy clears and the woodcock have moved out, I switch to IC and modified and reach for size $7 1/2$ shot in a 1 oz. field load.

You may not want to copy my methods because I have never shot a five-bird Michigan limit with five shells, nor have I ever bagged an honest double—one when both birds tore through the air at the same time. But I almost did it one day, when it would have really counted, in full view of two witnesses. I killed the first bird on a left-to-right blur as he tried to exit the canopy of bare aspen whips, then swung back left, the violent roar of more wings in my ears, to miss his partner quartering away. Oh, for a third shell!

Nobody shoots consistently well at grouse, at least no one I know. Sure, every gunner has his day, but is usually undone the next day or the one after that. The more a man

Top: Point! This Brittany has locked up on a grouse, but because today's bird is also a runner,
the grouse may be a city block or more in front of the dog. (Photograph - Tim Leary)
Bottom: Field or target loads of 7 1/2 or 8 shot are best in dense cover like these broomstick aspens. (Photograph - Henry Zeman)

brags about his grouse shooting prowess, the harder truth strikes when the string of hits becomes a roll call of misses. A good friend of mine once came to my grouse camp in the upper peninsula, fresh from bagging a hundred doves in Kansas.

"What's to it?" he asked, that first night in camp, shortly after his arrival. "A bird is a bird."

Yes, and a grouse is a grouse. The next day he shot a box of shells and missed every bird except one woodcock.

More than any other gamebird I know, grouse have an uncanny ability to twist through cover, always managing to keep a birch or maple between them and the shooter. Generations of dodging hawks in hot pursuit have honed the grouse's test-pilot skills. His sharp eyesight and wide field of vision allow him to keep one shiny eye on you and the other on a jungle-thick escape route without flying into trees. I read somewhere that ruffed grouse have the lightest skeletons of all the grouse species. Is that why they play the aerial acrobat so well?

Ever walk by a treed grouse, only to have the bird rocket out the back door when there is no possibility for a shot? A grouse can make himself look so slim, you may have thought he was just another branch, if you saw him at all.

A grouse's violent flush, wings banging like a gang of roofers, can throw an imaginary fist in your throat. But grouse can also fly so silently, your jaw may drop and you will wonder if you saw the bird or not. In Vermont, Tim Leary and I stood on a frozen country road high in the Green Mountains as twilight deepened around us. A full moon—the Cold Moon, according to the *Farmer's Almanac*—was just clearing a distant hill when suddenly a grouse, wings cupped and fan spread, zipped by soundlessly within ten feet.

"Did you see that?" I asked Tim.

"I'm not sure."

Grouse Dogs and Other Hunting Partners

I believe strongly in hunting grouse with dogs although I acknowledge that many hunters do not. Some of them are efficient predators who enjoy the hunting game as much as those of us with four-legged partners. My dogs make me look good. They find cripples and dead birds that I short-mark. They clue me to the imminent flush, prolonging that wonderful hair-trigger tension we hunters live for. They tell no one when I miss, and they provide cornsilk-smooth ears to stroke at night. I hunt grouse with an efficient little Brittany named

Because they can withstand cold weather and the fact that they represent generations of selective breeding, English setters are the most popular dog for hunting ruffed grouse. (Photograph - Maslowski)

Reggie; an older yellow Lab, Holly, who is of late growing very white in the face; and a young, cocksure English setter.

I picked up Dunstan, the setter, in Maine on the New England portion of my travels. He is supposed to fill the enormous space left by Lady Macbeth, who died unexpectedly, about three months before I hooked trailer kennel to motorhome and headed west. One advantage that dogless hunters enjoy is not having to bury their partners.

Most of the places I seek grouse get pressured by other hunters. As a result, birds that have survived the scattergun have learned some of the escape tactics their savvy farmland cousin, the ringneck pheasant, uses. Unless you hunt him in wilderness, today's supergrouse will run and flush out of range; skulk low to cover, then flush after you pass; or refuse to flush at all, leading you to believe the cover is barren. The best grouse dogs, both flushing and pointing breeds, are those that know how to sneak with moving grouse. Lately, my Brittany has been teaching me not to whoa him when on momentary point. "Let me go, Boss," he seems to say when his bratwurst of a tail begins quivering. "I'll nail him again. You come too."

Dogs *do* make a difference (in North Dakota, upland bird dogs were banned during the 1920s and 30s). The solitary hunter without a dog has one hand tied behind his back. He will not be able to step through all the birdy parts of a cover without grouse sidestepping him or running away to flush out of range. Another hunter ups the odds tremendously, because the partners can pinch grouse in fingers of cover and along the edge. Running birds must keep tabs on the crunching cadence of two predators. Employing the hunting tactics of stop and go and zig and zag will unnerve them into the air.

Driving and posting is a good method to try when covers are manageable. The technique works in farmland woodlots of the Midwest, aspen copses in the mountainous west, and gone-to-seed apple orchards of New England. But it is a waste of time when covers are too thick or too big.

In southern New York, six of us split into two teams to hunt 180 acres of prime grouse cover—upland hardwoods and conifers and lowland tangles of brush around a small

Top left: The early and mid-season grouse gunner has the advantage of finding woodcock in very nearly the same covers as ruffed grouse. (Photograph - Tom Huggler) Top right: Both flushing and pointing dogs that are trained can handle grouse efficiently. This is an English setter. (Photograph - Ron Spomer) Bottom: Ruffed grouse are hunted in 39 states, and the birds are now found in 42 states. Hunting with a good dog can spell the difference between success and failure. (Photograph - Tim Leary)

plantation of Christmas trees. The property owner, a deer hunter, watched ours and the grouses' antics from the vantage of his tree stand. He laughed while birds ran out of range, flushed, then hit the ground running. Several dashed underneath his tree stand to safety.

We regrouped the next morning. Choosing a ten-acre patch of brush that we knew was full of grouse—or so fresh tracks in the snow indicated—we posted four hunters at field edges. Another hunter and I and two of my dogs plunged into the shirt-shredding tangles. I kept the dogs close, and we zig-zagged to ferret birds from as many hiding spots as possible. But the thick habitat made for slow going, and that gave the grouse every opporunity to sidestep our drive and double back unseen. Only one bird flushed over one of the posters, who promptly missed. "Damn New York ringnecks" I wrote in my notebook.

Grouse Hunting Camps

I love to hunt grouse, alone with my dogs, or in the company of other hunters. But the gunner of grouse is an evolutionary creature, and his attitude changes the older he grows. One of those changes is realizing how important good dogs, good guns, good covers and good friends are to the sport. In recent years, several of us have set up an old-fashioned grouse hunting camp in the upper peninsula. Frost on the tentfly on a morning in October is an experience you cannot get in a motel. Coffee poured from a big enamel pot to a porcelain mug tastes better than the Seven-Eleven stuff in a styrofoam cup. Even without the benefit of running water or electricity, for a few precious days each October, twelve of us eat Sauteed Grouse Breast ala Marinade, Woodcock Tarragon with Wine Sauce, and other gourmet meals.

Every year, it seems, a new recruit is initiated to the passions of grouse hunting. Our oldest member is 80; he was General McArthur's aide de camp, and he tells good stories. Grouse hunting camp is the highlight of each hunting year for me. Two yellow leaves of aspen, stuck to windshield wipers, tells me it is too long between Octobers.

Colonel Gerald Graham and Dave Mull talk about their success on woodcock while grouse hunting in the upper peninsula.
(Photograph - Tom Huggler)
On following pages: Camp is the right place to reconstruct the day's hunting stories. (Photograph - Randy Carrels)

Iceland

Greenland

Alaska

Canada

Pacific Ocean

Atlantic Ocean

United States

Sharp-tailed Grouse
(Approximate Range)

*"If you hunt sharptails long enough,
eventually you begin to yearn for the country along with the grouse."*

—John Barsness

The Sharp-tailed Grouse

A cold wind is just right for hunting prairie grouse. Not the howling, hell-bent-for-leather blow that picks off a man's cap from his head. Or that inflates an empty game pouch like some airfield windsock. Just a decent breeze that makes the nose weep a bit in November and embarrasses uncovered ears.

Aldo Leopold said books about nature seldom mention wind because they are written behind stoves. But if you hunt plains grouse, surely you know about the kind of wind that moans in shotgun tubes while you look over the muzzles and lope for a setter turned to stone.

Too much wind stands the dog off from too far away. Then the birds are up at the edge of range and you are not confident of your shots, even though you have chosen the full-choke barrel and shoulder-slugging loads. A gusting wind is no good either because it delivers the vagaries of scent and confuses the dogs. Busted coveys and bad language result.

A steady wind, like the kind Dan Nelson and I got up on Lake Sakakawea near Garrison, North Dakota, is best. We walked a glacier-carved bluff in a place where September had rusted the little bluestem. Far below, Lake Sak wrinkled toward us, pushed by the southeast wind.

A single grouse was up before we knew it, his queer **kuk-kuk** sound floating downwind from 50 yards out. Too far for a shot. I tugged low the visor of my hunting cap so that I could follow the bird's flight. On strong, prairie-bred wings, he stroked and glided, stroked and glided over an immense field of combined wheat. At the end, the wheat stubble rode a hill in swirls of alternating tan and reddish-brown. Farmers plant the contours this way to check erosion, and the resulting pattern looks like the rich grain of a finished wood.

The grouse became a speck over the hill and disappeared. "He might go another half-mile," Dan said, reading my thoughts.

"Let's walk it anyway."

Enroute, we shot two grouse from a flock of 20. They erupted into the wind from native prairie fronting the wheat field. Dan got on them first, tumbling an adult bird with a 40-yard shot. Several others, probably juveniles, flew right at me. I killed one and missed one.

Nelson, who has hunted North Dakota sharptails most of his life, figured the grouse would head for a shelterbelt a half-mile away. He said they would set down there or in ditch cover near some buffaloberries farther on.

They chose the ditch. Rousing them there from waist-high weeds reminded me of pheasant hunting and in-the-face flushes, but it seemed odd to be shooting at brown and white birds that looked like hen pheasants.

Dan took our last grouse with a long poke beyond what I thought was the limit of range. When he finally brought the bird back, I noticed the cold and the wind had increased and Dan's ears were red.

Hunting Tactics for Sharptails

That incident in 1986 was my first successful hunt for sharp-tailed grouse. During my travels I returned to North Dakota to hunt near Bismarck and Garrison, and I found the wily sharptail in Montana, too, in the northcentral bench and coulee country below the Highwood Mountains, and farther east on table-top flat ranches near Grass Range. I hunted them unsuccessfully in Nebraska on September 15, opening day, when the 90-degree heat cooked us and the shrunken crops. The place was the High Plains, not far from the South Divide where, "When it rained 40 days and 40 nights, it got only a quarter-inch," or so said one of my companions, a native Cornhusker.

Earlier, I had shot sharptails from South Dakota cornfields when the wind battered the papery stalks and in Nebraska's Sand Hills, a place where time stepped out of bounds thousands of years ago. The birds utterly outwitted me in Michigan's upper peninsula the only time I hunted them there.

With or without a dog, sharptails are as wonderful to hunt as ruffed grouse. Parker Gillmore, an English sportsman who traveled all over the word in search of upland game,

Flushing dogs are perfectly fine for hunting sharptails. This Chesapeake Bay retriever belongs to Bill Wood of Bismarck, ND. (Photograph - Tom Huggler)

long considered pheasants to be "the noblest game bird that ever I had pulled a trigger upon." But when Gillmore encountered the prairie grouse of North America, he changed his mind. "What days of pleasure have I had in the pursuit of pinnated grouse," he wrote. "He is truly a noble bird, and affords the best of sport."

Returning to North Dakota, I experienced one of those days of pleasure. The buffaloberry crop was heavy in the draws between soft green hills, especially in the bottomlands where moisture had gathered. The hills reminded me of the Galway region in western Ireland, another land with timeless qualities. The buffaloberry clumps were on fire with red fruit, and the sharptails were loathe to leave the shaded grocery store. We shot them, one man to each side of the burning bushes, as the birds exited on command, like blue rocks from a spring-loaded trap. I made a mental note to carry a pocketful of rocks if I ever did this alone.

A Mandan proverb says that when the buffaloberry is heavy on the bush, a tough winter is coming. That is because the berries remain on the boughs deep into the cold season to provide food for grouse and other birds. Crops of the birds we shot that day looked like a Christmas stocking full of red candy.

The hunter will never get closer to sharptails than in September when family members feed together and take shade in clumps of willow, chokecherry, buffaloberry or man-planted shelterbelts. Then, young birds will hold for the dog, at least some of the time, and shots are reasonably close at 20 or 30 yards. This game of checkmate changes, of course, in November when the grouse are flocked together into groups of 25 to 100. On the short, open prairie, it is sometimes impossible to get within shotgun range.

Waiting along the edges of crop fields for sharpies to arrive at first light and again late in the day is a good way to hunt them. A better way—one that is more enjoyable, anyway—is walking them up, into the wind, a retriever at heel or, better yet, a pointer stitching an imaginery seam across the undulating prairie in front of you. The prairie is never as flat as it appears, and grouse often lie on the lee side of a slope just over the edge. Approaching into the wind helps conceal your noise and aids the dog in making game.

You will usually hear sharptails long before you see them, and that is because of the sentry bird. Like Canada geese, sharptails post a sentry when at rest or feeding, especially if the dining table does not afford a good view of their world. One time, Dan Nelson unsuccessfully tried to stalk a flock of sharp-tailed grouse that had settled into a

Top left: Sharptails flock together in fall and winter. These birds are feeding on buffaloberry shrubs. (Photograph - Ron Spomer)
Top right: This Montana sharptail dined on dandelions and a single sand cherry. (Photograph - Tom Huggler)
Bottom: Sharptails prefer the shade granted by buffaloberries during the hot early season.
A good crop furnishes food well into the winter. (Photograph - Tom Huggler)

sunflower field. Perched atop a tall plant, the sentry, swaying like a flagpole sitter in the wind, cried the alarm.

It is a strange feeling to look up suddenly and see 50 birds in the air, to hear their **kuk-kuk** cries everywhere. When that happens, you will flinch every time a hunting partner clears his throat or the breeze stirs a windmill vane a half-mile away.

Two hunters can work in tandem, one posting and one driving, to bring wary birds to bag. When I hunted with Mike McClelland in the Sand Hills, we followed a flock of sharptails after jumping them from a turnip field where they had been feeding. The birds flew only a half-mile, a short distance for November, and landed in bare trees next to a country church. A hundred years earlier, a buffalo hunter might have sneaked behind the same hill I did. Eventually Mike flushed the birds over me for easy shots.

Grouse jumped in the early season may fly only a couple of hundred yards before setting down again, especially if brush or heavy weeds are available. We have also put them aloft at close range late in the day when they are preparing to roost in such cover. I have read that sharptails will snow roost in deep drifts to survive howling nights of 50 below, but I have never seen them do it because, thankfully, I have never been caught on the prairie during a blizzard.

Some hunters insist the birds do not run but rather will squat in the grass until flushed or danger passes. To the contrary, I have witnessed sharptails try to sneak off, their heads low to the ground like that artful dodger, the cock pheasant.

In the early season, I choose improved cylinder and modified choke for my over and under and stuff field loads of 7 1/2 shot into my hunting jacket. Later in the season, I switch to modified and full choke and reach for copper-plated 6s because the birds flush more wildly and have more feather protection. Even so, sharptails require little punch to ground, and few birds are lost because of their open habitat.

Adults weigh about two pounds each and are 16 to 18 inches long. Their feet are feathered to the toes. The sexes look alike, their mottled brown-and-white overall appearance resembling a hen pheasant. Central feathers on the short "sharp" tail are actually squared on the end. On the male, these feathers exhibit a parallel striping; on hens, they are mottled. Feathers on the upper sides and back are mostly brown. The underbelly is white, but the light-colored chest feathers are punctuated with black Vs.

Top: The Sand Hills of Nebraska, home to both sharptails and prairie chickens, is the nation's largest undisturbed grassland region. (Photograph - Tom Huggler) Bottom: When male sharptails display, they often look like taxiing aircraft. (Photograph - Ron Spomer) On following pages: Prairie chickens often share the same range with sharptails; however, the two species have special habitat needs that differ. (Photograph - Tom Huggler)

Sharptail Range and Habitat Needs

At one time sharptails lived over most of the northern half of the continent, and their range extended as far south as western Oklahoma, northern New Mexico, most of Colorado and Utah, and northern Nevada and as far east as Illinois. Today, they are mostly gone from marginal habitats. The current range includes the northern Great Lakes and Great Plains regions, most of interior Canada from eastern James Bay to the Rockies and north into the Yukon and Northwest Territories, and on into central Alaska.

Sharptail bones excavated from a settlement dating to 2200 B.C. in McKenzie County, North Dakota, indicate the birds were an important food source for native Americans. Huge numbers of sharptails lived in the upper plains states at the time of settlement, prompting a schoolteacher traveling from Fargo to write:

"The grass that year was more than two feet high. Prairie chickens (sharptails) were thick. When we went out for a drive, as we sometimes did, the wheels of the vehicle or the horse's feet often crushed their eggs. I hated to see the wheel come up, dripping egg yolks. That wonderful grass waved like a sea in the sunlight, a forerunner of the wheat fields that would wave there in after years."

Lewis and Clark, and later, Audubon, noted large flocks of sharptails, and Theodore Roosevelt had plenty of them on his Elkhorn Ranch in the North Dakota Badlands. "The sharp-tail prairie fowl is the most plentiful of the feathered game to be found on the northern cattle plains," he wrote, "where it replaces the common prairie chicken so abundant on the prairies to the east and southeast."

Biologists have identified six subspecies. The plains race, found from northern Alberta south through North Dakota, is the most abundant. The prairie race inhabits most of Manitoba, eastcentral Saskatchewan, western Ontario, and the upper Great Lakes states where they have suffered severe habitat loss. It is extinct in Iowa, Illinois and southern Michigan.

Also in trouble is the Columbian sharptail, with most of the remaining birds living in British Columbia. In the past 40 years, the Columbian race has disappeared from Nevada, California and Oregon, and numbers are too low in Washington and Utah to permit hunting.

On the other hand, subspecies in Alaska, the Northwest Territories and the northern prairie provinces are in good shape. That is largely because 50 to 90 percent of their habitat remains unchanged by man.

Top left: Single sharptails often hold well for dogs. This setter is pointing a bird in sagebrush and grass. (Photograph - Ron Spomer)
Top right: Sharptails also have sharp eyes. Their excellent eyesight and strong wings protect them from plains predators.
(Photograph - Ron Spomer) Bottom: Wide-open shots are possible on sharptails, providing they flush within shotgun range.
(Photograph - Dave Books)

Sharptails are hunted in Canada and Alaska, North and South Dakota, Nebraska, Montana, Idaho, Wyoming, Colorado, Minnesota, Wisconsin and Michigan. North Dakota, where up to 40 to 50 birds may occupy a square mile of suitable habitat, has the best hunting.

Sharptails are native to the shortgrass prairie and the northern plains. They like wide-open spaces, and the minimum amount of land required to manage them effectively is about four square miles. Farming, which brought the prairie chicken west from the tallgrass prairies of Illinois and Iowa, did so at the expense of sharptails. They are most plentiful where their habitat has remained undisturbed. The birds fare less well on prairies and plains that have been grazed, and they succumb quickly when too much land is broken by the plow. Drought also has an adverse effect on them.

On the other hand, the species apparently is not subject to the mysterious cycles that affect ruffed grouse, which they follow in popularity among hunters.

Gone are the buffalo and the native tribes and the sodbusters' crude homes of logs and earth. The vault of sky remains. And remnants of virgin prairie sweep. And a speckle-bellied bird that brings endless delight to those who seek him.

North Dakota has the nation's best sharptail hunting. The author photographed this scene in September near Lake Sakakawea.

Iceland

Greenland

Alaska

Canada

Pacific Ocean

Atlantic Ocean

United States

Prairie Chickens
(Approximate Range)

"Our genesis was in grassland;
perhaps our Garden of Eden was prairie."

—John Madson

The Prairie Chicken

Cassoday, Kansas. The sign along state highway 77, the Prairie Parkway, declares a population of 120. My 1981 highway map, which, admittedly, is eight years old, says 119. Well. At least, the self-proclaimed Prairie Chicken Capitol of the World has not lost any people.

What it has lost is prairie chicken hunters. "The Lions Club used to feed breakfast to 1,500 of them at the grade school," said Norma Arsenault, who owns the Cassoday Cafe. "They slept in the gym, too."

I had stopped at Norma's cafe for the $3.75 hamburger steak dinner. Tomorrow was the first Saturday in November, the traditional opener of Kansas' prairie chicken hunting season.

"I'll be in here at two tomorrow morning getting breakfast ready for 400 hunters," Norma said.

I looked around at the half-dozen tables in the little restaurant, which dates to 1879, and wondered where 350 of those hunters would sit.

"There will be standing room only," Norma smiled, reading my thoughts. "Many of them will eat in their cars. Main Street will look like a campground. You ought to come back in the morning."

I couldn't. My destination was Elkhart, a long way away in extreme southwestern Kansas. Elkhart is closer to the state capitols of Santa Fe, Denver and Oklahoma City than it is to Topeka. But I planned to return to Cassoday and the Flint Hills, where I had hunted for greater chickens before, later in the week.

I stood up to pay my bill. "How come the Lions Club doesn't sponsor the breakfast anymore?" I wondered.

"We got old," said a man named Chet, who had come into the cafe earlier with his

daughter and two grandsons. Chet moved to Cassoday in 1938, but he hadn't said why or from where. "And some of the hunters spoiled it for everybody by going on land they shouldn't have."

Outside, a train rumbled by on its way to Strong City. Chet turned to look at the grandsons.

"That's Uncle Jim's train," he said. "That's the Santa Fe. Uncle Jim brings it through here all the time."

The boys looked at each other and smiled.

"You come back again," Norma said as I walked outside to the boardwalk and past two hitching posts that were weathered gray. I wondered if prairie chicken hunters had tied their horses there a hundred years earlier.

Prairies and Chickens

Prairie chickens may be the oldest grouse in North America, at one time occupying much of America's waistband as well as southern provinces of western Canada. There are four subspecies. The original range of the greater prairie chicken, which was and is the most abundant, was mostly confined to the 250 million acres of tallgrass prairie. At the time of settlement, the ocean of grass stretched from the eastern Great Plains through the upper and lower Midwest to Indiana and southwestern Michigan. Tendrils of it reached into Ohio, Tennessee and Kentucky.

Father Marquette recorded the first prairie chicken from the Great Lakes region when a member of his expedition shot one during the winter of 1674-75 near present-day Chicago. When settlers crossed the Appalachians, they found prairie chickens to be as abundant "as sands of the seashore," or so an early observer wrote.

Exploding in number behind the plow, the birds quickly spread to new areas. By the end of the nineteenth century, their range included southern portions of the prairie provinces, eastern Montana, Wyoming and Colorado and northern Michigan where, along with sharptails, they set up housekeeping on openings created by military airfields.

But the expansion was short-lived because as more and more prairie was turned over to support small-grain cultivation, chicken numbers tumbled. They have been virtually eliminated from areas where the conversion from grass to cropland exceeds 60 percent.

Overgunning by market hunters and sportsmen alike also helped do them in. The hunters followed their pointing dogs and were chased in turn by groaning game wagons. The

Top: Cassoday, Kansas is the self-proclaimed Prairie Chicken Capital of the World. (Photograph - Tom Huggler)
Bottom: This lesser prairie chicken male was photographed on a shortgrass gobbling ground. (Photograph - Ron Spomer)

storytellers say the chickens (and sharptails) rose in an ever rolling curtain as flock merged into flock. A sharp-eyed shotgunner could count on killing 50 to 100 per day.

Apparently, prairie grouse were as limitless as the buffalo. In 1874, an estimated 300,000 chickens were shipped from eastern Illinois alone. Chicago restaurateurs paid $3.50 to $4 per dozen, dressed. In New York City, chickens fetched twenty cents per pound. One shop sold 2,400 birds daily during the 1878 Christmas holiday season.

Eastern Kansas, which includes the Flint Hills and its vast bedrock of chert and limestone, contains the world's largest remaining population of greater prairie chickens. Included in this region is the 25,000-acre Nation Ranch, the largest existing stand of tallgrass prairie. Enough chickens are left in Kansas, Nebraska, South Dakota and Oklahoma to allow hunting.

Small remnant flocks are holding on in Illinois, Missouri, Wisconsin, North Dakota, Colorado and Minnesota. Meanwhile, the roll call of extirpation grows longer: Michigan, Ohio, Kentucky, Iowa, Arkansas, Texas, most of Canada.

A second race is the lesser prairie chicken, which is recognized by some as a separate grouse species. It occupies semi-arid grasslands of sand-sage and shin-oak bluestem prairie. Lessers, too, spread behind the plow for a few years and then succumbed to row cropping and livestock grazing. Limited hunting is allowed in shrunken portions of the original range: southwestern Kansas, the Oklahoma and Texas panhandles, and eastern New Mexico.

Man has impacted the environment of the prairie chicken more than any other grouse. The heath hen subspecies, living along the barren coastlands from Massachusetts to Maryland, became extinct in 1932. The endangered Attwater prairie chicken, whose home used to span some seven million acres of Gulf Coast prairie in Texas and Louisiana, is nearly extinct. Less than 2,000 remain from a former population estimated at one million.

What will become of the prairie chicken depends upon what man decides is important. In a delicate balance, it is possible to have crops and beef and birds, provided the grassland is not drastically altered.

If history repeats itself, though, the birds will lose. The Flint Hills is a good example of what can happen. Burning the prairie at three- to five-year intervals revitalizes it, but annual charring, which is presently occurring on 85 percent of the Flint Hills, can be disastrous to chickens.

Still, there is some hope. Greaters are actually expanding in the northcentral portion of the Flint Hills. Through the use of remote-sensing photography, biologists now know the precise balance of five land cover types that will increase the number of lesser chickens.

A greater prairie chicken male calls from a rock in spring. (Photograph - Gary Zahm)

More good news: A booming ground was found in southwestern Saskatchewan in the spring of 1987. The government there and in Alberta is studying a reintroduction plan. North Dakota, where chickens once thrived, has swapped sharptails for Kansas chickens and is raising them on the Arrowhead National Wildlife Refuge. They have been successfully reintroduced in Oklahoma and Wisconsin.

Hunting Techniques

"To the oldtimer no other bird can quite take the place of the prairie chicken," wrote Col. Charles Askins in *Game Bird Shooting*. The colonel should know: He hunted lessers and greaters in several states 100 years ago when the huge flocks wavered like heat shimmers under the grassland sky.

Recommended guns, loads, chokes and hunting tactics are similar to those for sharptails. You either post grainfields in the early morning or late afternoon or you walk the prairie in hopes of jumping birds within range. Early in the season is a perfect time to hunt alfalfa fields containing grasshoppers. The crop of a lesser chicken I killed near Ashland, Kansas, contained an unbelievable 73 grasshoppers. I know because a friend and I counted their heads.

The grainfields are best late in the season when grasshoppers have frozen out for the year. Sometimes chickens will ignore the grains altogether if enough native food exists. Lawrence Smith, with whom I hunted in southwestern Kansas, recalled one winter when lesser chickens foraged on wild sunflowers miles from any grain field.

Some hunters set up hay bales on field edges at strategic places and then hide behind them. There is no guarantee that chickens will land in the same part of any grain field day after day. You play the hunch game, but if you have enough friends along, someone will get shooting.

A few miles and a few days on the prairie will put it all together for anyone who strides after these birds. Hunting with Lawrence taught me to look for stands of native prairie—indiangrass, big and little bluestem, wheatgrass, buffalograss, switchgrass—that have not been heavily grazed by cattle or recently mown and baled. Ten- to 24-inch-high fields are best, especially upper hillsides and crowns containing berries or broad-leafed weeds. On warm days, chickens will sit along these high spots to cool off, or they will squat in the shade of shrubs if there is no wind.

Even so, be prepared to trek until your hip sockets ache, because you may have to walk miles between flushes.

Holly retrieves a greater prairie chicken from milo stubble in Kansas. (Photograph - Tom Huggler)

Chickens like to loaf in cover that gives them a good view of the country. Their excellent vision qualifies them as the pronghorn of the grouse world, and they run on their wings at the first hint of danger. Lawrence and I found them along gentle slopes where yellow seams of grama grass wove in and out of an artist's palette of subtle hues—coppery sand love, gray sage, bright green yucca, rusty bluestem. Prairie chickens live in lovely places.

On that opening weekend, I shot two limits—four birds. On Monday, I took two more while posting an alfalfa field 100 miles east near Ashland, Kansas. I did not deserve those last grouse—having blown a certain double by trying to pump the stock of my over and under. That was because the pair of chickens roared by overhead like darting teal, and I suffered a momentary flashback to duck hunting in a marsh with a pump gun.

Anyway, six birds are enough when you know there are so few. I should not have felt guilty. Later, farther east again in Kansas, I shivered for three days while curled up on the frozen prairie along the edge of a milo field while waiting for a greater chicken to find my shotgun pattern so I could get the bird mounted.

I won't soon forget the morning I collected him. Bill Harmon, a friend of mine from Durham, Kansas, had been scouting the birds for days, awaiting my arrival.

"I've got 'em marked," Bill said, as I climbed the stairs to the second-story bedroom of the Harmon home. "They're running the buffet table. Green shoots of winter wheat in the morning. Soybeans and milo in the afternoon. Pleasant dreams."

Pleasant dreams meant sleep, which was not likely, given my state of expectations.

Next morning in the dark we walked into the wheat field. I took one side of a hay-bale round; my partner, Ron Spomer, chose the other side. Setting up nearby was Kent Becker, an official at the Durham State Bank, where he would be wearing a suit in an hour, open for business. Kent said he might get in an hour's hunt after closing that afternoon.

Yes, chickens do their level best to be accommodating. It isn't their fault they can be ridiculously easy or frustratingly difficult.

Daylight began to brighten over anvil-shaped clouds hugging eastern hills. Ducks flew overhead with a whoosh of wings that sounded like shower water. At exactly 30 minutes before sunrise, quail began calling, followed by the raucous crowing of cock pheasants. A widgeon whistled as it went by; the chickens, skylighted, were right behind.

Top left: These greater chicken males were caught fighting on a gobbling ground. (Photograph - Gary Zahm)
Top right: Many a young hunter's first prize was a prairie chicken. (Photograph - Tom Huggler).
Bottom: A chicken hunter slakes his thirst while his tired partner naps. (Photograph - Ron Spomer)
On following pages: Chicken hunters are no different than other grouse hunters—they all have excuses for missing. Author listens to Mike Smyth explain how to miss. (Photograph - Ron Spomer)

I stood up, promptly lost the birds against the dark earth, and missed twice while little jets of flame erupted from my gun muzzles. "There goes my chance to bag a greater chicken," I moaned to my partner.

For some reason, I received another chance, knocking down a bird from a second, smaller flock. Holly, my yellow Lab, lunged after the chicken. When I killed another, also a handsome male, I unloaded my gun.

Chicken Characteristics

The birds I turned over and over in trembling fingers looked like the books said they should: overcoat of barred brown and black feathers, undercoat of brown chevrons across a chest and belly of buff to white. Both sexes have pinnae, which are feather tufts along the neck, but the male pinnae are longer. The tail of both is fan-shaped but short. In the cocks it is mostly black; in the hens it is heavily striped. Central tailfeathers resemble a small brush dipped in white paint.

Tympani (air sacs) of the greater chicken are orange-colored when the birds display in spring. They are rose-colored among lesser chicken cocks, which are about 25 percent smaller in body size than greaters. Overall, the lessers are similar in appearance to greaters, except they are a little lighter in color.

"In all of modern America, there is no more lost, plaintive, old-time sound than the booming of a native prairie chicken," wrote John Madson in *Where the Sky Began*, his tribute to tallgrass prairie.

I have yet to hear that sound. Lawrence Smith says lesser cocks on the leks make a noise like percolating coffee from the old Maxwell House TV ad. Greater males sound like wind blowing over a bottle.

In flight, however, they may cackle with a *tucka-tucka* noise. One morning while waiting for legal shooting time, I listened to lessers make a *cluck-cluck-cloo* sound that reminded me of bobwhite quail. The notes were liquid and bubbly and sometimes they were mixed with prolonged clucks. I have heard chickens squeak and squawk and gabble, and I have heard them laugh.

But that is only when I miss, then try to pump the rigid forearm of an over-and-under shotgun.

Top: Chickens are plentiful enough in a few states to warrant hunting. Unrestricted market gunning a century ago contributed to their demise in some places. (Photograph - Gary Zahm) Bottom: The author's tired Labrador fell asleep after a successful hunt for greater chickens. (Photograph - Tom Huggler)

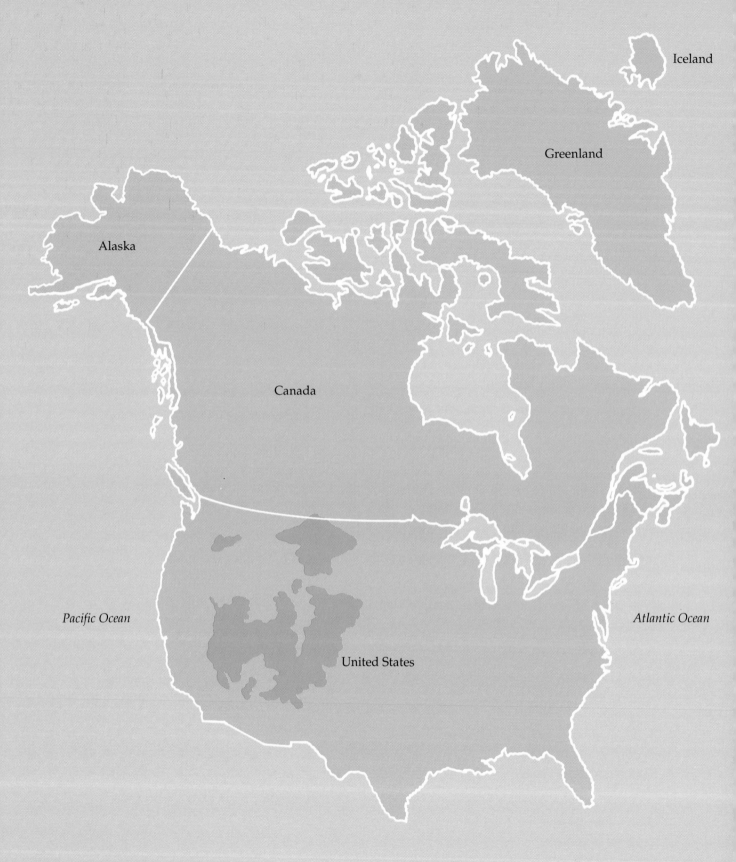

Iceland

Greenland

Alaska

Canada

Pacific Ocean

Atlantic Ocean

United States

Sage Grouse
(Approximate Range)

*"I could draw a map today of each clump of red bunchberry
and each blue aster that adorned the mossy spot where he lay,
my first partridge on the wing. I suspect my present affection for
bunchberries and asters dates from that moment."*

—Aldo Leopold

The Sage Grouse

If you hunt birds, you may know all about bird-hunting maps. Sometimes they are scrawled on cocktail napkins in the blue haze of smoke-filled bars. Sometimes they are scratched into the dirt by pointed objects such as rocks or sticks. A government cartographer had drawn this map, a topographic representation of the rugged Shirley Basin in Wyoming. Then, another mapmaker—a hunter—had added crude pencil marks to show where he had recently seen flocks of sage grouse.

The second artist goes by the name of Harry the Harvester.

"We call him that because he knows all about sage grouse," said Chris Madson, my hunting partner and host. "Harry says about 400 birds are using these areas on the map."

How would a man know where to go without such a clue? Roughly two-thirds of Wyoming, or some 58,000 square miles, is blanketed by 13 species of sagebrush. Sagebrush is the wonderful stuff where thunder chickens eat, sleep, hide and make love. Thunder chickens? You can call them bombers or sage hens or sage chickens, too. They are still the biggest grouse in North America.

I gazed out over the enormous alkaline flats, past the miles of rolling gray-green sage to the outcroppings of the Shirley Mountains. The outcroppings were a rust-iron red, and they were parched. Only four inches of rain had come to the basin; already it was late September and not much time was left to get eight inches more, a normal amount of rainfall in one year. I licked my dry lips.

"Tell Harry the Harvester thanks," I said.

"We haven't found his birds yet."

By the time we did locate sage grouse, late in the afternoon, frustration had replaced

my normal optimism. My legs felt like they had been drawn and quartered from miles of hoofing it up and down endless coulees and from chasing my Brittany who insisted he could run down an antelope. And the wind that was blowing 40 miles an hour had scrambled the shutter curtain on my camera. The camera was ruined.

Rules to abide by when hunting sage grouse:

1. *Always catch a dog before he gives chase.*

2. *Turn your back to the wind before attempting to reload a camera.*

3. *Remember that sage grouse are never as close as they appear and that they fly faster than they seem.*

When I did get a chance to bag a thunder chicken, I blew it—an easy double on two bombers that burst from the sage in front of me. That feat so impressed my friends that I repeated it five minutes later.

That night in camp I brooded while eating fried strips of young sage grouse, but they were not birds I had killed. Chris and our other hunting partner, Ron Spomer, contributed the game. My donation was a can of whole-kernel corn.

Sage Grouse Myths

Sage grouse are not as big as many people think. A large bird is five pounds, and the average weight is only three to four pounds. Sage hens are never heavier than when they are on the leks in spring. A study in Montana showed that adult males then averaged 6.3 pounds and hens averaged three and one half pounds. In Wyoming, cocks in spring weighed five to seven pounds; females, about three to three and one half pounds.

Some claim that sage grouse are as big as young turkeys. Not true. Nor are their wings larger, at least in proportion to body length, than the other grouse species. A single flattened wing averages a little more than 12 inches long or about one-half of the bird's body length. That ratio is fairly equal among all the other species of grouse.

For some reason, these and other myths get perpetuated when stories are told about sage chickens. The meat is not inedible; in fact, I found it to be very good, especially slices of breast fried medium rare, which is the same way I like beefsteak. Teddy Roosevelt, who gunned sage hens in North Dakota, knew as much. "It is commonly believed that the flesh of the sage grouse is uneatable, but this is very far from the truth," he wrote in *Hunting Trips of a Ranchman.*

A large sage grouse will weigh five or six pounds, but they are actually smaller than many people believe. (Photograph - Michael Francis)

Thunder chickens are not always found in the heaviest sage around either. In fact, most of the time, they prefer cover short enough to see over. But it is true that they can be hard to find. After Chris and Ron left, I spent two more days hunting alone in the vast basin. I saw lots of antelope but no sage hens.

Are the birds dumb? Certainly not as dumb as the way I have performed when hunting them. No grouse species would have survived on this planet if it had little intelligence. Sage grouse may be *naive*, but expose them to two-legged predators a time or two and they grow cagey fast. They do appear clumsy when they first take to wing, but that may be because the sexes fly differently, thus giving the illusion of awkwardness when you see a flock pumping aloft. The larger males hold their bodies parallel to the ground, while the hens rock from side to side.

A hunting book published in 1944 that I read recently insisted that dogs have to develop an anti-alkaline nose before they can hunt sage grouse effectively. Don't believe it. Once my Brittany realized he couldn't catch a pronghorn, he had no problem smelling grouse. And by all means, take a dog with you, in spite of the admonition of some who claim that you can't get close to birds with one.

It is true that sage grouse grow nervous around animals that remind them of coyotes, but that is also true of sharptails and prairie chickens, which no one argues should be hunted without dogs. Besides, dogs help to find downed thunder chickens in dense clumps of sage.

In Colorado, we hunted them behind fluid shorthairs and my frenetic little Brittany. In Wyoming, we used more Brittanies and a wide-running setter. In Montana, we relied on a yellow Lab, a golden retriever and a viszla. Many young-of-the-year grouse, programmed no doubt by their mothers to freeze when danger approached, held for the pointers. I can't imagine hunting sage grouse without a dog, but then I feel that way about gunning any upland bird, whether the quarry is a six-ounce bobwhite quail or a six-pound bomber.

Sage grouse are certainly different than those furtive, secretive quail, though. A whistling bobwhite says, "Here I am. Find me." A sage grouse, his dark head periscoping above a bush, says, "Here I am. Try to sneak up on me." As long as the bird can keep an eye on you and your dog, he is not afraid. Walk 10 yards toward one, and you will see why: The bird will sidle off 11 yards. Run at him and he will fly away.

Top: Our biggest grouse, the sage hen lives in a land of big vistas. (Photograph - Ron Spomer)
Bottom: Ron Spomer and his U-shaped setter, Tillie, move in on sage grouse point in Wyoming.
Rarely do sage grouse allow dogs and hunters to get so close. (Photograph - Tom Huggler)

Hunting Methods That Work

The best way to hunt sage hens is to treat them like the big game they are. Scouting as though you were after mule deer or turkeys, look for tracks, feathers and droppings. Triple-toed prints along roads and around watering holes are positive signs, along with droppings the size of .45 caliber casings. Piles of the brown-and-white droppings indicate a roost, but because the scat dries out rapidly and might not deteriorate for months, it may be hard to determine how old it is.

Use binoculars to save on boot leather and sore muscles. Alfalfa fields are good places to glass in early morning and late afternoon, especially in September when grouse fly or walk there to feed on grasshoppers. Midday haunts may be stock-watering tanks, irrigated fields or the damp bottoms of coulees. After a hard rain, the birds will perch on low rocks in the sage in order to dry off. Sage hens also loaf in low-growing brush, and in pockets of grass within the sage. These may double as roosting sites, especially if the surrounding sage is higher than the grass and the spot is on a south-facing slope. You can stake out a roost in late afternoon or waylay morning birds coming to feed and water.

If you spot grouse during the day, plan a stalk into the wind. When hunting with a partner or two, resurrect the old squeeze play where one man posts and the other drives. Keep an eye out for flocks of sage grouse heading to food or roosting areas. Although I have never witnessed it, friends of mine in Nevada and Colorado tell me they have followed bunches of 100 or more birds for miles as they drift along in a loose circle a half-mile or so above sagebrush flats. When the birds land, the hunters drive to within a few hundreds yards and then stalk them.

Although I've never heard of anyone doing it, hunting bombers from horseback might be worth a try. Why not? Other friends of mine in Kansas have ridden for prairie chickens while their dogs, big-ranging Brittanies, rocked and rolled across the plains. And Dakota hunters besides Teddy Roosevelt have gone horseback after sharptails.

The Importance of Sagebrush

Hunt in sagebrush and you will carry its sweetly pungent aroma on your trousers for hours. The scourge of farmers and ranchers, sagebrush belongs to the genus *Artemisia*, 300 kinds of which live throughout the world's temperate zones. These fragrant shrubs, in one form or another, have been around longer than most other living things. Some 60 million years

Top left: Chris Madson and his Brittany took this sage grouse in Wyoming. (Photograph - Tom Huggler)
Top right: Dryland habitats necessitate the booting of hunting dogs. These are English pointers. (Photograph - Tom Huggler)
Bottom: Sage grouse droppings are much larger than those of other grouse. Dry climate, however,
makes it difficult to age the sign. (Photograph - Tom Huggler) On following pages: Dave Wickham and Dick Dixon look over rolling
sagebrush/rangelands in Colorado. The region yielded both sage and blue grouse. (Photograph - Tom Huggler)

ago, an Old World ancestor, perhaps a wormwood or mugwort, established itself in North America. Pollen studies indicate that by the Miocene epoch of 15 to 20 million years ago, *Artemisia* was widespread throughout the semi-arid West.

Sage grouse, which may have evolved from either forest or plains species—taxonomists don't agree—cannot live without sagebrush. They eat its leaves, year around, supplementing their diet with insects and alfalfa leaves in summer and early fall.

When Lewis and Clark saw their first "cock of the plains" in Montana in 1806, sagebrush, in one form or another, occupied upwards of 400,000 square miles of what was to become 11 states. The plant ranged from Canada to Mexico, from California to the Black Hills. The war on sagebrush began when the first farmer tried to carve out a cropfield and found that the plant did not plow very easily. The rancher learned that sagebrush increases, not decreases, when it is moderately grazed by cattle.

Besides plowing and grazing during the past 100 years, burning, rotobeating, chaining, railing and spraying are weapons man has used to eradicate sagebrush. On one 12,000-acre area in Wyoming, a five-year spraying program with 2,4-D wiped out the entire wintering population of 1,000 sage grouse. By 1951, more than 50 percent of the bird's original habitat had been eliminated. That is why the Audubon Society has added sage grouse to its Blue List of species whose population is declining because of overall habitat loss.

Prairie chickens are the first of the remaining grouse species to face the threat of future extermination. Sage grouse, whose populations are cyclical, are next.

Actually, their numbers hit an all-time low during the droughty years of the 1930s but have rebounded remarkably since. Sage grouse are currently plentiful enough to warrant hunting in nine states. Wyoming leads the nation in harvest, followed by Idaho, Montana, Utah and Nevada. Small numbers are also taken each year in Colorado, California, Oregon and North Dakota.

Characteristics of Sage Grouse

I saw my first sage grouse in Colorado when one jumped up in front of my Brittany. I don't know who was more stunned—the dog, the bird or I. The bird was black and white in color and was unlike anything I had ever seen. But it flew like a grouse, and so I killed it, and Reggie made a proper retrieve. One of my hunter partners that day was Dick Dixon, who

Sage grouse hunters often have to put in long miles in hot, dry climate. This scene was photographed in Wyoming's Shirley Basin. (Photograph - Tom Huggler)

owns a sporting goods store in West Vail. Dick came over to inspect the grouse. It was a nondescript brown overall with white underwings and brown and black markings on the back.

"It's a young bird," he said, feeling the sharp breastbone. "Probably a male. See the bit of black on the throat? Adult males have a lot of black there. Here are the yellow eyecombs, too." Dick, who has hunted sage grouse for more than 20 years, then stuffed the bird in the game bag of my vest. I was used to toting ruffed grouse and more recently blue grouse, which are about the same size as ruffs. But this bird filled the cavity.

"And they grow larger?" I asked.

"Much larger."

Ten minutes later I found out how large when Dave Wickham, the other member of our party, shot a perfect double, and one bird was a mature cock. But it looked so diferent than photos I had seen of displaying males in spring, their horsecollar of white feathers puffed out like a cartoon senator about to filibuster. But the bird was a male—separating the white breast feathers near the esophagus, I spotted the loose skin of olive green indicating the air sacs.

Sagebrush is the stuff of the West. Traveling east on U.S. 2, I saw the last clump of it on my western itinerary near Rugby, North Dakota, the geographical center of North America. That seemed appropriate. The day before, I had seen my last sage grouse, actually 15 of them, about 400 miles farther west in Montana. That seemed appropriate, too.

It was dusk and three of us were bouncing along a dusty two-track road, coming off a ranch where we had been hunting sharptails and sage chickens all day. We spun around a corner, and, there, loitering near the road like a gang of street-corner punks in black-leather jackets, were several grouse. They looked surly, hanging around there and stretching their thin necks to look us over. They certainly didn't act worried.

While I fumbled to uncase my gun and stabbed my pockets for shells, the pack slowly walked away. I opened the door and gave chase; naturally they had the audacity to fly when they were 30 yards beyond range.

On the walk back to the truck, I bent down to retie my boot. I noticed my pants smelled strongly of sage.

This young shorthair made acquaintance with a porcupine in Colorado— and paid the price. (Photograph - Tom Huggler)

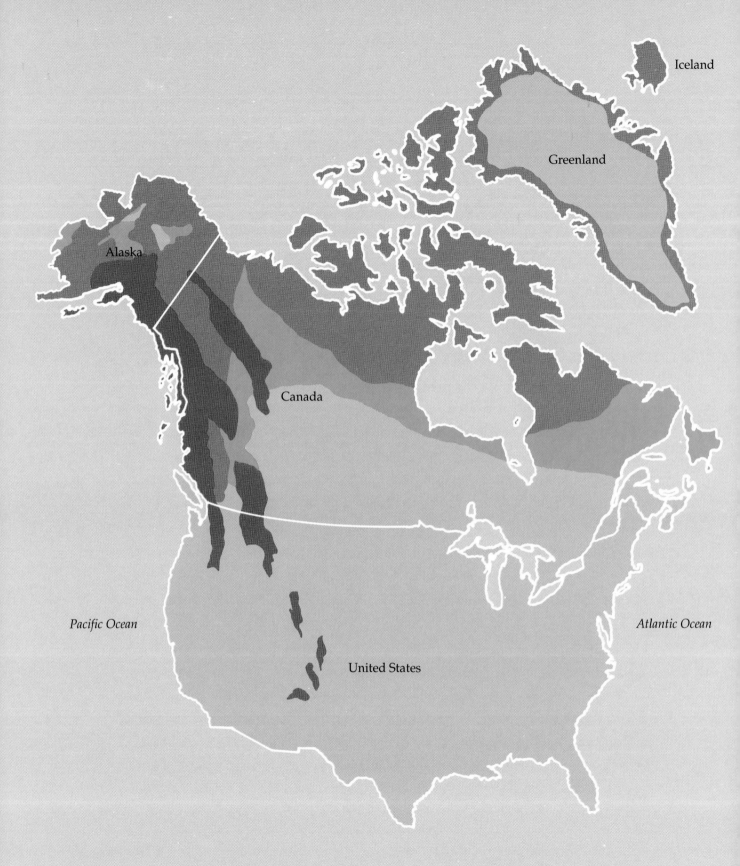

Iceland

Greenland

Alaska

Canada

Pacific Ocean

Atlantic Ocean

United States

Ptarmigan
(Approximate Range)

Rock Ptarmigan
White - Tailed Ptarmigan
Willow Ptarmigan

*"In ptarmigan shooting there is absolutely nothing artificial.
You and nature are on the same plane, with nature often taking the upper hand."*

—Robin Macdonald Rolfe

The Ptarmigans

Ptarmigan live in some of the world's loneliest and loveliest places. They are North America's least hunted and most ignored upland gamebird. Probably 99 percent of the continent's snow grouse, as ptarmigan are sometimes called, have never heard the report of a shotgun, and that is because most hunters do not go to the places where ptarmigan live. Those that do go are usually after bigger game.

I speak from personal experience, having seen my first ptarmigan while hunting moose in the Kuskokwim Mountains of central Alaska. It was September; Autumn had already brushed the aspens yellow and was starting on the tundra, staining it with bold reds and burnt orange. I was sneaking through low-growing willows along the Post River drainage in a place where spectacular mountain peaks towered.

The willows before me now suddenly quaked, and a dozen brown-and-white birds hammered up and away. They were willow ptarmigan, also known as willow grouse, and some of them cackled in the manner of prairie chickens and sharptails. The ptarmigan flew like other grouse—flap and glide, flap and glide—out over the burning tundra.

I pointed my rifle, a 7 mm bolt-action model crammed with 160-grain Nossler partition bullets, but wished I was shouldering a shotgun. Later that day, armed with a Winchester 20 gauge, I saw a fine bull moose. That's the way it goes on an Alaskan hunting trip.

I did not shoot a ptarmigan that fall, but I certainly learned some things about them, most importantly the places where they live. I found willow grouse in broad alluvial valleys where the moist tundra supported dwarf birch and any number of the 25 species of willow that grow in Alaska. Ptarmigan love blueberries, crowberries and bearberries—I

found those, too—but their main diet is the thumbnail-size leaves of willow and birch. They pick and choose which ones to eat.

Later, while hunting caribou on the Alaska Peninsula, we camped on the tundra next to the Cessna 185 Skywagon that brought us there. Each morning, male ptarmigan served as our alarm clock, their loud gutteral cries of **go-back, go-back** gathering the flock for breakfast just before sunrise.

I have both read and been told that it is easy to kill a ptarmigan with a rock or a .22 caliber revolver. I believe it because at times these birds appear absolutely fearless. On other occasions, though, they grow spooky, just as all grouse do when they feel threatened. Will Troyer, a freelance writer and Alaskan native, has hunted ptarmigan for 30 years, mostly with pointing dogs. He counts willow grouse among his favorite upland gamesters, and he has practically the whole state to himself and the few friends who hunt with him.

In an article appearing in *Wing & Shot* magazine, Troyer wrote: "I am a wilderness man and prefer hunting in the wilds of Alaska. It is an overpowering feeling to be alone with a good dog in a remote mountain valley filled with ptarmigan, knowing there is no other hunter within many miles."

It *is* overpowering.

Species and Distribution

Six percent of the earth is tundra, which gives snow grouse lots of remote places to live. I have flown over more ptarmigan country in Alaska and northern Canada than I will ever be able to hunt in my lifetime, but I have also walked enough of the spongelike tundra to know that it is not as devoid of life or beauty as many people think. Devoto was right: there is no such thing as uninteresting landscape.

Scientists have classified 44 subspecies within the three identifiable races or species of ptarmigan. The rock ptarmigan is a high arctic bird with a northern limit of about 83 degrees N. latitude. The home range of these snow grouse lies well above the Arctic Circle and includes most of Ellesmere Island and Greenland—the upper limits of earth's real estate. There are 23 subspecies.

The other two ptarmigans probably evolved from the rock ptarmigan or a close ancestor. The willow ptarmigan is a subarctic tundra grouse that, like the rock, is circumpolar. Sixteen subspecies live in Siberia, Mongolia, Scandinavia and Scotland and Ireland. In North

This hunter is glassing for ptarmigan in Alaska in the fall. Wide river valleys featuring lots of dwarf willow and birch are good places to hunt.
(Photograph - Tom Huggler)

America the willow ptarmigan thrives throughout Alaska and northern Canada, including Newfoundland. In winter this species may migrate as far south as central Canada from the Pacific to the Atlantic.

The white-tailed ptarmigan is an alpine bird found only in North America. It ranges from central Alaska and the Yukon Territory along the western half of British Columbia to the Cascade Mountains in Washington. Scattered populations are extant in the Rocky Mountains from Alberta to Colorado. In the lower 48 states whitetails occur in Colorado and Montana, and they have been reintroduced to New Mexico, California, Oregon and Utah. Our smallest grouse, five subspecies of white-tailed ptarmigan have been identified.

Characteristics of Ptarmigan

A friend of mine, Paul Banyas, once shot all three species of ptarmigan in a single hunting day in southcentral Alaska. Thanks to his training as a wildlife biologist, Paul was able to identify the birds. All have feathered feet to the toes, and the upper tail coverts extend to the tips of their tails. Those are the key differences between ptarmigan and the other grouse species. Besides its smaller size, the white-tailed ptarmigan has an all-white tail. The rock and willow grouse feature dark tails. Both of those birds are similar in appearance and are about the size of ruffed grouse, but the willow is a little larger than the rock, which sports a black line through the eyes to the beak.

Ptarmigan turn all white in winter. In summer, they are piebald with white bellies and brownish chests, backs and upper wings. The brown of willow ptarmigan is a rich chestnut color, but it is typically a beige or tawny color among rock and white-tailed species. Males of all species (and the white-tailed female) sport bright red eyecombs in spring.

The ptarmigan's world is a fragile one, and life is a tenuous prospect. Aerial and ground predators plunder egg, chick and adult. An estimated 60 to 80 percent of first nesting attempts fail, and the growing season is so short that ptarmigan dare waste no time if renesting is to be successful. Some try it three times and fail three times.

For these reasons, the ptarmigan is wonderfully adapted to its environment. To elude predators, chicks have little or no body scent, and they are perfectly camouflaged to their habitat. A day-old rock ptarmigan chick I photographed in the Northwest Territories while on a fishing trip was identical in color to the lichen-covered rocks on which it posed. Without ever moving, the chick would disappear whenever I looked away.

Top left: All ptarmigan races have feathered tarsi to the toes. (Photograph - Tom Huggler)
Top right: This willow grouse is wearing its early autumn plumage in spite of snow conditions. (Photograph - Tom Huggler)
Bottom: This rock ptarmigan chick was photographed in the Northwest Territories. Note how the bird's cryptic coloration matches rocks and lichens. (Photograph - Tom Huggler)
On following pages: A male willow ptarmigan calls from his perch in spring. (Photograph - Will Troyer)

Hunting Traditions

Ptarmigan are hunted hard in some parts of the world. The Norwegian National Field Trials are held on willow ptarmigan each year. In Scotland, the Glorious Twelfth (August 12) is the opening day of the red grouse (willow ptarmigan) hunting season. It is one of Britian's most celebrated events. I happened to be in Edinburgh one summer a couple of days before August 12, and the newspapers and sporting shops were buzzing with news and commentary about the upcoming hunting season. Two hundred fifty miles south, London restaurants were competing to see which establishment would be the first to serve the delicacy.

This sport is not for those with frayed pockets. During my visit, I stopped at John Dickson & Son, Est. 1820, a famous sporting goods store where business was brisk in anticipation of the Glorious Twelfth. An assistant on the shooting side (there is also an angling department) was momentarily free. He wore a dark blue summer suit. Horn-rimmed glasses circled friendly eyes.

"Help you, Sir?"

Odd. This was university English with no rolling of the Rs. "I'm wondering about that 12-gauge double," I said.

"Ah, yes, a fine fowling piece. One of a matched set. This is the 12 bore. Care to shoulder it, Sir?"

I leaned into an imaginary crossing shot. "How much?" I asked.

"Twenty-five thousand pounds (about 40 grand, at the time). For the pair, Sir, of course."

Of course. Trembling, I lowered the gun, certain it would crash to the floor at any moment. I grew acutely aware of my jeans and tennies. Even if I *could* afford such a gun, I would not have been able to find a place in Scotland to hunt with it. One must have reservations well in advance on the farms and shooting estates where red grouse are managed and hunted.

The lovely highlands of purpling heather host both walk-up and driven shooting, hunting tactics that are more than 100 years old. Groundskeepers manage the moors for grouse, as they have for generations. The burning of heather to improve habitat dates to 1859, about the time the English were inventing the double-barrel for the purpose of shooting driven birds.

Walk-up hunting with dogs may be affordable because one ghillie (guide) accompanies a brace of shooters. Driven shooting, however, which involves beaters and

Top: Ptarmigan are the continent's least-hunted grouse, yet they may be the most abundant. These are white-tailed ptarmigan. (Photograph - Ron Spomer) Bottom: Hen willow ptarmigan with chick. (Photograph - Maslowski)

loaders, is definitely not affordable for most. During my visit, an Edinburgh newspaper told of a Saudi Arabian prince who shelled out $20,000 for a one-day driven hunt. Such sporting diversions are relative, of course, in terms of cost. I severely warmed my gun barrels once in Spain on a driven hunt for red-legged partridge. The fee was $1,000 per gun. Yes, it *was* worth it.

Hunting Opportunities

You can gun these same red grouse in Alaska for the price of a $60 nonresident hunting license. The limit is a generous 20 birds daily and 40 in possession, and the season is long—from August 10 to April 20. Canadian limits range from five to 10 ptarmigan daily, depending on the province or territory. Few hunters take advantage.

During my travels for grouse, I did not want to spend the time or money to journey to Alaska, but I did want to collect a ptarmigan. Colorado was the logical place to go. It and Utah are the only states of the lower 48 with a hunting season.

If you want to hunt alpine white-tails as I did, you have to go above the fluttering gold of high-country aspen. You have to go above the black pine and, higher still, beyond the stunted spruce. You have to go to the boulder-strewn saddles and to the cirques with their alpine meadows of dainty flowers, and sometimes you have to go to the caprock itself.

I went to the caprock at about 13,000 feet, but I wish I had been better prepared. I live at 600 feet above sea level. Even though I worked out a little in the summer and was in fairly good shape, there is no way for the body to produce more red blood cells, which it does at higher altitudes, than to go there. To help thin my blood, I ate aspirins for a week and fed them to my dogs as well. Even so, I suffered a bit from a bloody nose and a lot from terrible headaches, the kind you get about noon after the restaurant waitress has poured you caffeine-free coffee all morning by mistake.

Later, I learned that the headaches are caused from excess acid in the blood, which is also a byproduct of staggering around at high altitudes. The cure? Eat antacids, a roll at a time.

The Colorado hunting season for white-tailed ptarmigan was September 9 to October 8. The earlier I went, the better my chances of finding birds before snow plugged shut the mountain passes. Getting to the places where snow grouse live is the hardest part of hunting them. They occupy an estimated 4,000 square miles of mountain habitat in the Colorado Rockies, but not every peak and saddle has birds.

A white-tailed male ptarmigan in spring plumage walks across a boulder in alpine habitat. (Photograph - Ron Spomer)

I budgeted four days and finally succeeded in scratching down one ptarmigan with two hours left in the afternoon of the fourth day.

September 15, 1989:

The motorhome looked like a Tonka toy far below while I stopped to pant, using the excuse to glass the mountain walls of gray, green and purple. Snow-covered crags towered above sapphire lakes tucked away in the dark clefts of spruce. Two miles to the south of my position, I watched my partner, Dave Wickham, and his two shorthairs making slow progress across an immense snowfield. Nothing else was alive, not even the little white shapes that my seven-power binoculars tried to convince me were ptarmigan but were only small white rocks.

The wind was blowing and my hands felt cold. I wished I had worn gloves. I wished, too, that I had brought a sling for the gun. This would have freed up my hands in case I took a spill, a likely occurrence if the going got any rougher. My yellow Labrador had not left my side since we started our ascent, up the scree slope, down into an alpine draw, and back up the crumbling other side. Higher and higher. One slow step at a time, stopping every 100 yards to catch our breath and swallow down a headache so bad it was making me squint.

Holly drooped next to me, her sides heaving and her tongue out. Reggie, younger and with better lung capacity, loped down the hill toward us, then lay on his back, a clear sign that he was having fun and would greatly appreciate a tummy rub. I felt like cuffing him.

Cottonwood fuzz drifted across the slope, as barren of vegetation as the 50-yard line on a football field in late November. A butterfly reminded me that certain peaks in the Rockies produce some species of butterflies that live no where else in the world. I hoped ptarmigan lived here, too.

The dogs and I went on, higher and higher. If a grouse lived anywhere in this rarified air, he would live here, I remember thinking upon reaching the top of a cirque and looking down into an oasis of green as bright and manicured as a golf course. Boulders the size of golf carts perched along the fairway where patches of scrub willow joined bits of snow. A stream flashing in the sunlight trickled its way through what looked like lush watercress. We started down.

I saw the grouse tracks in a skiff of melting snow and, forgetting my throbbing temples for a moment, began to follow. A minute later Reggie ran the brown-and-white bird out from under a rock. I remember thinking it was too small for a ptarmigan, and why weren't

Top: These white-tailed birds are in their autumn plumage. The Rockies are in the background. (Photograph - Ron Spomer)
Bottom: The author glasses high-country saddles and slopes for ptarmigan. (Photograph - Tom Huggler)

the feathers all-white? Reggie sight-pointed, then began to creep. The bird looked back once and rocketed into the air. I swatted him back with a load of 8s.

A moment later I cradled in hand the bird that Reggie retrieved. It was a ptarmigan all right—the feathered tarsi proved as much—but it seemed so small, weighing perhaps a pound and rivaling a barn pigeon in size. Apparently we had caught the grouse in its summer wardrobe—white wings and tail, gray-brown head, neck and upper back. I slipped the warm bird into a nylon stocking to keep its plumage intact during the hike back down the mountain to show Dave.

My headache never returned.

Tracks such as these led the author to a ptarmigan high in the Rockies. (Photograph - Ron Spomer)

Iceland

Greenland

Alaska

Canada

Pacific Ocean

Atlantic Ocean

United States

Blue Grouse
(Approximate Range)

*"Each year these contracts with game animals are renewed, rewritten.
Each year you grow older and there are new terms."*

—**Barry Lopez**

The Blue Grouse

I can thank a coyote for helping me bag the first blue grouse of my 30-year hunting career. Two friends and I were packed in the cab of Dick Dixon's pickup truck, waiting for a high-country shower to end and sharing precious space with each other and Dick's 90-pound black Labrador retriever. Speedy, the Lab, appeared to be winning the Battle of the Legs as he maneuvered his thick body between us and insisted upon stretching his coal shovel of a head onto my lap.

We were parked along a muddy trail on a private ranch west of Vail in Eagle County, Colorado. Like most September storms in the high country, this one passed quickly. An Indian summer sun began to penetrate the swirling, gray-bellied clouds. Soon, Dick was able to point out the Wasatch, the Gore and New York ranges, along with Castle Mountain.

Meanwhile, my leg, trapped under Speedy's weighty head, had gone to sleep.

Four other dogs, belonging to me and Dave Wickham—the third member of our group—whined and shifted impatiently in the truck camper. Maybe they had smelled the coyote. We watched him a hundred yards off, a tag-rag animal with shaggy coat and spindly tail. Nose to ground, he drifted like yellow smoke through the clumps of low-growing sagebrush. Suddenly, the coyote tensed. Four birds shot into the air a dozen yards in front of him.

"Grouse!" Dick said. "Blues. Maybe there's one or two that didn't flush."

I opened the door, and Speedy nearly fell out. The coyote lined off through the green sage and did not look back.

Gun loaded, I limped to the spot where the birds had flushed. Dick certainly knew his grouse: A single battered up from the sage, and I killed the bird cleanly with a dose of 7 $\frac{1}{2}$ shot from the under barrel of my 28 gauge.

Over the years, I had seen blues on many other occasions but had never hunted them. On Vancouver Island and on mainland British Columbia, where I camped with my family in summer, broods had walked through our campsite. While mule deer hunting in Colorado one October, I watched a blue grouse stare at me for an hour from his conifer perch thirty feet over my head. He alternately gawked and strutted with all the confidence of a city pigeon on a window ledge.

Those experiences, plus what I had read and been told, led me to believe that blue grouse were fool's grouse. "Unsporting," the stories said, unless you were armed with pistol, slingshot or bow. The habitat where they lived was supposedly so dense that if a bird did flush, it was only to land in one of many nearby trees where you were certain to bury your shot if you tried, like a good sport, to take the grouse in the air.

The bad reputation that blues have been meted out is not altogether fair. Whenever I ran into them on my grouse hunting travels, I found these birds to be challenging targets and, in some cases, as tough to claim as the most gun-shy ruffed grouse. Consider what happened after I slid that single, my first blue, in the gamebag.

With dogs buttonhooking ahead, we three hunters fanned out through the rolling sage, which was spliced here and there with bunchgrass and bouquets of yellow flowers that I could not identify. In a little while, a hillside clump of shimmering aspen took shape before us. Dick skirted left, Dave stepped right, and I bore straight on into the cover. Recalling my ruffed grouse hunting experiences, I was thinking this was a birdy-looking spot when I heard frenzied wingbeats to my left. Two blues busted out in front of Dick, who promptly emptied both barrels of his side by side. The untouched pair flew 200 yards before disappearing behind a groundswell in the sage.

We never saw those grouse again.

I was halfway through the aspens when a single flushed somewhere behind me, then appeared as a number eight station blur in the window of blue sky over my head. I don't often hit that shot, whether the target is clay or feathers. Close behind my vain salute, Dick's shot centered the bird. Feathers drifted down through the yellow aspens.

Running out of trees, we spread out again and continued downhill through the sage. Soon, Dick killed a single that flickered out along the slope to his left. Then my Brittany nosed out two more blues; I killed one and pulled feathers on the second. Moments after that,

Reggie and I look over Colorado habitat. We found blue grouse in sagebrush and pockets of aspen like those in the background.
(Photograph - Tom Huggler)

Dave and I both missed on respective singles. By midmorning we had nine birds, which is the daily limit for three hunters. I took the last blue, an adult hen from a covey of 15 that we had broken earlier. That bird came right at me, head up and tail flaring and wings alternately pumping and gliding.

It is true: Blue grouse *can* supply all the sport a bird hunter might want. That discovery shattered one myth. A second myth vanished when I realized there were no conifers within miles of these heaving sagelands. Everything I had read insisted that blues are always found in or near evergreens, typically true fir or Douglas fir.

Migratory Habits and Habitat

Apparently we had caught the birds, several family units, still in their summer habitat. Blue grouse are reverse migrators, moving to higher altitudes in fall when most other migratory animals and birds drift to lower elevations. Why do blues go up instead of down? The reason is simple: Their winter diet is almost exclusively the needles, buds and seeds of conifers—namely fir, spruce and pine. Also, the dense evergreens provide escape cover and warmth. Because the birds are so highly adapted to this protective, food-supplying habitat, wintering losses may be only 20 percent.

On the other hand, ruffed grouse have been known to lose up to 70 percent of their numbers from fall to spring.

In the spring, the blue cockbirds move down the mountainsides and set up hooting territories in fairly open stands of trees or shrubs. Like those of ruffed grouse, their territories are only a few acres in size, and several cocks may occupy a small area. Generations of males sometimes display on the same rocks, logs, stumps, mounds of earth or from tree limbs. They may set up in one location or choose several different spots. Display antics involve fanning the tail, strutting, exposing colorful air sacs on the neck, and making hooting calls that sound like *oop-oop-oop*.

Males return to the high country after completing their reproductive chores. By late summer, hens and their broods also begin moving up the mountainsides, eating berries as they go. Juneberries, serviceberries, blackberries, wild grapes and currant are a few of their many preferred foods. By November, the birds are at timberline or even above it. Here they will overwinter until the urge to reproduce prompts them to descend again. Some yearling males follow dominate cocks to lower elevations. Others remain in the high country.

Top left: Hen (left) and male blue grouse. Note how much darker the male appears. (Photograph - Tom Huggler)
Top right: Dick Dixon shot this blue grouse in Eagle County, Colorado. (Photograph - Tom Huggler)
Bottom: Conifers near grass openings also produce blue grouse which are reverse migrators in fall. (Photograph - Ron Spomer)

Range of the Blue Grouse

Blue grouse range from the coasts of southeastern Alaska to northern California at altitudes from near sea level to several thousand feet. Blues of the interior occupy elevations from foothills to 12,000 feet. They live from the southern Yukon and McKenzie River region throughout British Columbia and western Alberta into the northwestern U.S. Home turf includes Washington's Cascade Mountains, southern Oregon and along the Sierra Nevada deep into California and western Nevada. Mountain ranges in Idaho, western Montana, Wyoming, Utah and the Colorado Rockies are all strongholds. Scattered populations live in Arizona and New Mexico ranges.

Each of the states and provinces mentioned have hunting seasons for blue grouse. Except for localized gunning pressure, the birds are greatly underharvested, even during years when the population cycle is at low ebb. The biggest threats to their numbers appear to be livestock overgrazing in the blues' lowland summer habitats, excessive clearcutting, and probably aerial spraying for insect control. Fires and small-scale timbering operations help improve blue grouse habitat by generating new growth and opening up dense forest areas and creating edges.

Biologists have identified eight subspecies. Coastal birds are often referred to as sooty grouse. The cocks exhibit yellow air sacs, and their eyecombs are smaller than dusky grouse whose air sacs are purple in color. The eye combs of both subspecies may be yellow, orange or red. Dusky grouse inhabit interior mountain ranges. Other common names for blues are Richardson grouse, mountain grouse and hooters.

Blue grouse are smaller than sage grouse but larger than ruffed grouse. In a Wyoming study, adult males averaged two and a half pounds for the year, and females averaged just under two pounds. The sexes are an overall slate color and appear similar to the casual eye. However, hens exhibit a dark brown or buffy mottling on the upper parts, chest and sides whereas the males are gray. Some neck and chest feathers are tipped with white, and the underwings, abdomen and undertail are white to light gray. When fanned, the dark tail usually sports a narrow band of gray or pale blue across the feather tips. Sometimes there is no band.

Hunting Techniques

Blue grouse grow edgey when hunted with dogs. The day after our sagebrush rangelands hunt, Dave Wickham and I labored to reach Saddle Mountain, high in the Vail Pass

This blue grouse was photographed in mid-September during the hunting season.
Some believe the flesh of the blue grouse is the best eating among all grouse species. (Photograph - Ron Spomer)

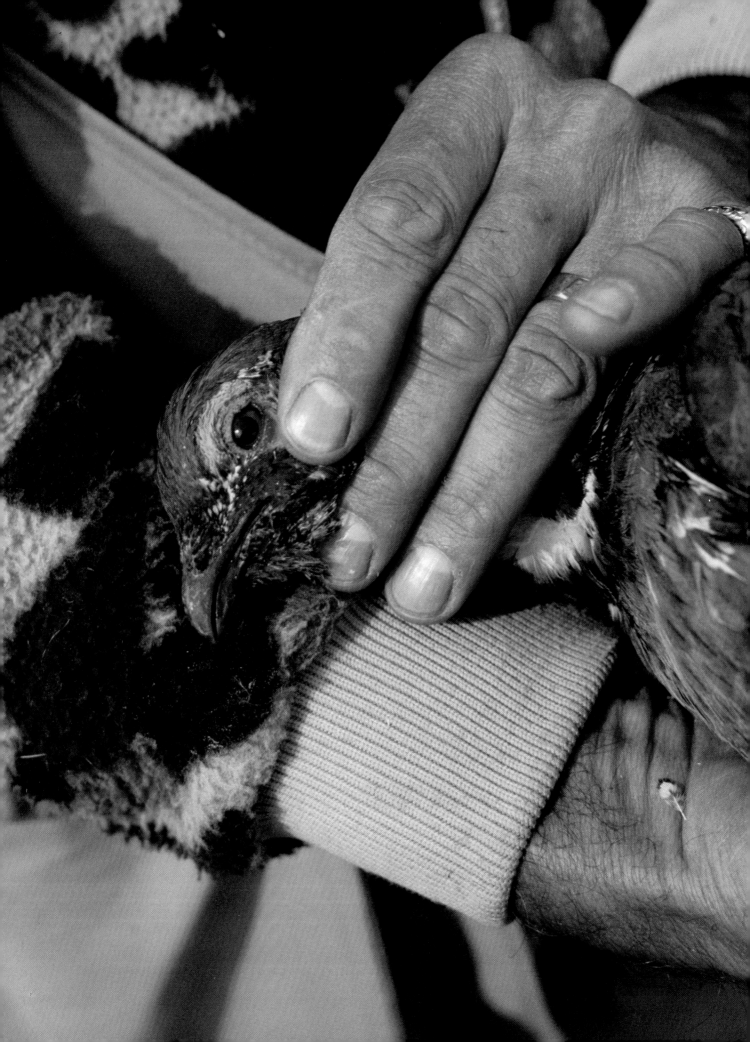

area. Our goal was to find a ptarmigan on the untimbered, snow-swept ridges at 11,000 to 12,000 feet, but first we had to trudge uphill through spruce bogs ringed by patches of black timber. The area looked like textbook blue grouse cover, and I was surprised and disappointed that we saw nothing on the arduous climb.

I was fast learning that blue grouse hunting (as well as ptarmigan hunting) is a bust or boom affair. Birdless and exhausted, we split up about four in the afternoon to begin our descent. Just below timberline I started following a set of fresh elk tracks in the melting snow.

Maybe you know, from your own field experiences, how tracks lead on to tracks. Suddenly, there they were—new grouse prints stitching their way through the alpine conifers. I called in my Brittany and yellow Lab, both of whom subsequently ignored (for some reason) what I knew had to be smoking-hot scent. Heeling the dogs, I followed the several sets of tracks for a few yards. Within a few minutes they turned into four nervous grouse, peering over a log that was half hidden under dense spruce boughs.

Reggie froze in a sight point, his stub tail quivering. Holly charged ahead for the flush. I figured the birds would rocket right to left. A bit of Windex-blue sky appeared within the steady gloom of spruce. Sure enough, the grouse went up in a collective roar. Swinging with them, I fired at the patch of blue as targets blurred, then kept swinging and picked out another bird flashing through a second opening farther on. Reggie and I both saw that grouse tumble through boughs to earth, and he leaped for the bird.

Meanwhile, Holly was delivering a dead blue grouse from the first shot.

Why is it that no one is ever around to witness such incredible feats of wingshooting? A few days later in Wyoming there was no shortage of spectators to watch me miss sage grouse after sage grouse.

The next time I ran into blues was in Montana after hunting them unsuccessfully in the Shirley Mountains of Wyoming. That's another odd thing about bird hunting, or any hunting for that matter. Hours of walking through miles of prime habitat may produce nothing but sweat rivulets between the shoulder blades. Then, without warning, the action is absolute and immediate. Birds up all at once. Gunpowder on the air. Mad-dash retrieves by the dogs. A warm bird in the hand, and it is over again within seconds of starting.

The eye comb of the male blue grouse is orange-yellow. During spring displays, it is much more prominent than this fall-killed bird (Photograph - Tom Huggler) On following pages: This blue grouse hunter was photographed in the Carson National Forest in New Mexico. (Photograph - Gary Zahm)

It began anew in Montana in the Helena National Forest near Townsend. The place was among gorgeous stands of limber pine on heart-attack hills featuring taluses of broken shale. The shale had spilled into surrounding ground cover of low-spreading juniper, lupine and six-inch-high grouse wortleberry. Again, classic blue grouse cover.

The altitude was only 9,500 feet, a snap for a sea-level man who has earned his lungs in the rarified air of the Colorado Rockies.

In four hours of hunting, two new partners and I flushed 20 blue grouse, nearly all of which were singles. We killed four and missed the others. Thanks to our dogs, the grouse were high-strung birds that flew hard and knew all about keeping trees between them and any line of fire we dared attempt. I tossed away a pocketful of shells on targets that darted in and out of cover as adroitly as any ruffed grouse. Only one blue landed in a tree, and we promptly missed that bird on the reflush.

Jeff Herbert, a biologist with the Montana Department of Fish, Wildlife and Parks, killed three of the four, all juveniles and hens. The other hunter, Steve Shimek, and I doubled on the fourth bird, a big male that tugged on my shoulders as he bounced along the mountainside in my gamebag. As I write this, that grouse is with a taxidermist in Bismarck.

It was only mid-September, but apparently the blues were at or near their wintering covers. Typical of grouse, they escaped downhill, and some of them flew a long, long way.

I thought about stumbling down that mountainside and trying to put them up again. And maybe again. It was possible, I supposed, to move them all the way to the lowland drainages and aspen pockets which Jeff said could be stiff with ruffed grouse.

Ruffed grouse?

Far below, those inviting aspen groves looked like flecks of gold in a sea of green.

You may not believe this—I know I wouldn't have—but the hunting for blues that day was far too good to worry about ruffed grouse.

Top left: Jeff ages a young bird for Steve by examining the primaries. Adult birds often exhibit rounded tips. (Photograph - Tom Huggler)
Top right: Flushing breeds such as this golden are better than pointing dogs for blue grouse hunting.. (Photograph - Tom Huggler)
Bottom: Blue grouse habitat includes conifers and some deciduous cover in altitudes from 5,000 to 12,000 feet. (Photograph - Michael Francis)

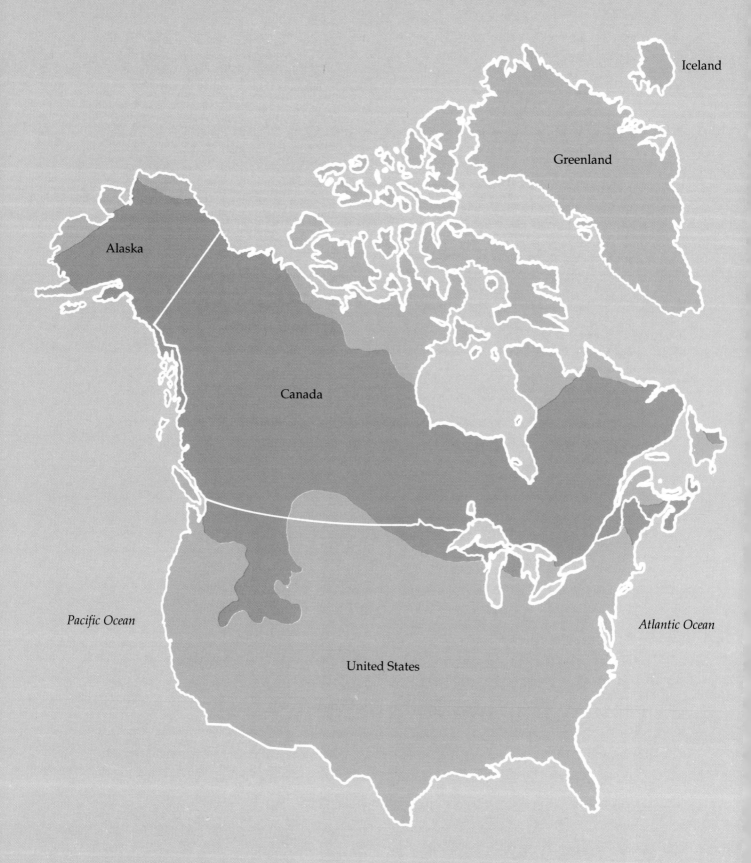

Iceland

Greenland

Alaska

Canada

Pacific Ocean

Atlantic Ocean

United States

Spruce Grouse
(Approximate Range)

*"Far from the road, you can discover a peaceful silence and sense the world
as it once was, and as it still is, in the realm of the spruce grouse."*

—William L. Robinson

The Spruce Grouse

The spruce is the dunce of grouse, at least from the hunter's point of view. Most of the 300,000 to 400,000 spruce grouse bagged in Canada, Alaska and the few northern states with hunting seasons are taken incidentally to ruffed grouse and other game. Many other swamp or black grouse, as the spruce is sometimes called, are potted with small-caliber handguns as the birds peck grit along the road or lounge in evergreens and gawk at armed passersby.

Because spruce grouse act so tame, few serious wingshooters seek them for sport. How excited can you become about gunning a bird that is trusting enough to eat berries from your hand? Or that flies from the ground to a nearby pine tree and refuses to budge again unless you jiggle the branch on which he sits?

"They sat upon the trees in flocks and were killed one after another without offering to stir," wrote Baron de Lahontan in *Some New Voyages to America* in 1703. Of course, de Lahontan could have been meant ruffed grouse or heath hens when he described the "woods hen."

The "fool's grouse" is also the court jester, both in dress and manners. The males in particular dress for the stage. In spring, they puff up with all the self-importance of any buffoon—the blood-red eyecombs flaring; black collar feathers erect; undertail feathers, white-tipped and bristling like spears; the broad tail fan with orange feather tips appearing and reappearing in card-trick synchrony. With chest swollen and step exaggerated, the cocks strut for an audience of one—an attendant hen. The spring pageant is, therefore, both colorful and comical. Display antics include other clownish behavior such as a dumb show of silent wing clapping, head bobbing, neck jerking, and flutter jumps into the air.

An easy target for two-legged and four-legged predators, how does the spruce grouse survive at all? In truth, he is not as silly as he seems, at least around natural enemies. He knows that death comes from the air in the form of hawk, falcon and owl and from the jaws of bobcat, lynx, coyote and wolf. He freezes at any hint of aerial danger, and he is quick to fly to the safety of a limb when stalked by ground predators. Losses of adult birds probably occur less frequently than with other species of grouse. One reason is the heavy screening cover of conifers where the spruce grouse lives. The other is that the birds concentrate less than other grouse.

Range of the Spruce Grouse

The spruce grouse's range is the northern boreal coniferous forest that spans North America from coast to coast. Scientists have identified four subspecies. They occupy much of Alaska and northern Canada from the stunted spruce boglands that sprinkle the tundra south and east across the Canadian Shield to the Maritimes and northern New England. The Franklin grouse subspecies lives from extreme southeastern Alaska through British Columbia and southwestern Alberta into northern Washington and Idaho, western Montana and northwestern Wyoming. The Canada race ranges across southern Ontario, dipping into northern Minnesota, Wisconsin and Michigan, and extending into the southern Maritimes and northern New England states. The Hudsonian subspecies lives throughout the rest of Canada and Alaska, except for the Valdez subspecies that occupies southern coastal Alaska.

Roughly nine percent of the earth's land is northern boreal forest, but the spruce grouse is native only to North America.

Because the spruce is a true wilderness bird, its overall habitat has been impacted less than the other grouse species. An exception is the Canada subspecies. Logging in the northern states a century ago removed much of the conifers upon which the birds depend. Spruce, fir, pine, hemlock or larch, mixed with some hardwoods, is crucial to their existence.

Loggers took the softwoods first, namely the prized pine, and then came back to level the hardwoods.

In the upper Great Lakes states and southern Ontario, spruce grouse nearly disappeared. In Michigan, the hunting season closed in 1913 and has not reopened since although spruce grouse are a fairly common occurrence in the upper peninsula and a few are seen in the northern lower peninsula. They are only rarely observed in Wisconsin. The birds

The displaying spruce grouse may be the most colorful of all North American grouse. (Photograph - Richard P. Smith)

have made a good comeback in Minnesota, increasing with the resurgence of second-growth forest about 50 years ago. There is no open season on spruce grouse in Maine, New Hampshire, New York, Vermont and Nova Scotia. They may be hunted throughout the rest of Canada and in Minnesota, Washington, Montana, Idaho and Alaska.

Spruce grouse are trusting, open, naive. Like any grouse that is not hunted, they have no fear of man, but they do grow nervous around dogs. When flushed, the birds will stretch their necks and fret from the safety of a branch while keeping a sharp eye on your dog and ignoring you completely.

An Alaskan Hunting Experience

We didn't have a dog along when Ron Spomer and I hunted spruce grouse in Alaska a few years ago. We were on the Haul Road north of Livengood and headed for the Arctic Circle and the Brooks Range. It was late August, and the tundra was beginning to glow with orange and red, the aspens with yellow. The aspen leaves, near-perfect circles with pale-yellow undersides, looked like punched-out confetti tossed to the dark forest floor. The all-gravel Haul Road, or Dalton Highway, as it is also called, is 400 miles long. As we drove along at 45 mph, a dust funnel spread behind our Jeep, and we could feel the steady swish of gravel under the floorboards. We fish-tailed around a loose corner where a road grader had piled high the stones. There, along the road shoulder, were eight or ten grouse-like birds pecking grit.

I slid the Jeep to a stop. My partner, who had been dozing, woke up and looked out the window. "What are they?" I wondered.

"I think they're spruce grouse," Ron said. Just then, the birds flushed into a band of nearby conifers. "Yes, they are spruce grouse. See the brown-orange tail band?"

We fished our 20 gauge shotguns from the mound of gear in the back seat. I was using a Winchester 101; Ron had brought along his trusty Citori. Dropping 7 1/2 shot field loads into the barrels, we each took a side of the evergreens where the grouse had alighted. When one nervous bird rocketed out, Ron shot him on the wing. The report spooked a second grouse into flight, and I killed him before he could land in another tree. The others did not want to exit the cloaking safety of the conifers. We shot three more.

Five birds were enough for a couple of meals. Returning to the Jeep, we replaced guns with cameras, then each shot a couple rolls of film of those grouse left in the spruce trees.

Ron Spomer shot this pair of young spruce grouse when he hunted with the author in Alaska. (Photograph - Tom Huggler)

We assumed this was a brood covey, although a rather large one because the average spruce grouse clutch contains only five to seven eggs. The young males exhibited black-tipped breast feathers; the females' were brown-tipped. Both sexes sported the pale orange tail band. The males carried a tiny slash of red above the eye. Checking the crops, we found a few small red berries—perhaps lowbush cranberries—a yellowish matter that we assumed was partially digested insects; smooth, bright-green leaves about the size of a shirt button, and a smattering of dark seeds the size and color of sesame.

Neither of us had eaten spruce grouse before. Ron boned the breasts, then dropped them into a skillet of sizzling butter. The meat was as delicious as ruffed grouse. Flesh of the juvenile birds was light-colored, much like the ruffed grouse. Meat of the henbird, though, was darker in color but also tasty.

Diet and Habitat

Like other grouse species in summer and early fall, spruce grouse are opportunistic feeders of insects, berries and other vegetable matter. Climax forests of evergreens provide screening cover from predators, but the birds also seek a nearby ground cover of bracken ferns, low-growing shrubs or reindeer lichens where they can forage and which they can see through. Blueberries, cranberries, whortleberries, foxberries and crowberries are a few of the many ripening fruits they love. By late summer, the birds also begin to consume evergreen needles, especially the inch-long dark needles of tamarack (larch), which fall to the ground with the onset of winter. Throughout the frozen months, the birds live exclusively on the needles of spruce, fir and pine. They must consume huge quantities because of the poor nutritional value.

Not much is known about the habits and life history of the spruce grouse, at least in comparison to the other grouse species. Although the birds are easy to observe and catch for banding and study, they live in wilderness, often apart from each other. Michigan studies by William Robinson show that although springtime densities of ruffed grouse may total 80 to 100 birds per square mile, 25 spruce grouse is a large number.

Hens typically nest at the base of a single conifer with low-spreading branches. Hatching of eggs occurs from May to July after an incubation period of 21 to 23 days. Like the blue grouse, spruce grouse chicks are able to fly in only a few days. They stay with the hen all summer, and, although the male does not participate in brood rearing or defense, he is often

Top: Proof of the spruce grouse's lack of fear of man is this male trying to mount a dummy hen as set up by researcher William Robinson of Northern Michigan University. (Photograph - Richard P. Smith)
Bottom: Both sexes of spruce grouse have orange-tipped tail feathers. (Photograph - Tom Huggler)

seen traveling with the family. One of the birds that stayed in the tree and allowed Ron and me to photograph him was an adult male.

Bagging a spruce was a low priority during my travels for grouse. Most hunters I interviewed that had shot spruce grouse did so incidentally or mistakenly when in pursuit of other birds. In Montana, my travel plans did not include the extreme northwestern part of the state where spruce grouse live. When I stopped in Duluth, Minnesota, to interview Gordon Gullion, the famous ruffed grouse researcher told me I was only a two-hours' drive south of the spruce's range. But a hunting commitment in Wisconsin precluded my going north at that time.

Knowing the Minnesota hunting season lasted until December 31, I figured there was plenty of time to bag a bird for my collection. The itinerary placed me in New England for ruffed grouse hunting experiences during the first two weeks of December. I would return home on December 16, then hop a flight for International Falls on the 19th. A wildlife technician with the Minnesota Department of Natural Resources offered to help me find a bird there.

"If you're crazy enough to come to the nation's cold spot to shoot a bird off a limb, I guess I'm crazy enough to help you do it," was his dubious offer.

The round-trip airline tickets cost $600. I choked down tears when I ordered them just prior to leaving for New England.

The worst December weather in a century slammed New England during my visit, and conditions worsened as I migrated from New York to Vermont to New Hampshire. My last hunt was on snowshoes in the White Mountains when the temperature was 20 below and my dogs were constantly chewing ice balls that formed between their toes. The hunting was rugged and what few grouse we found were snow roosting.

The combination of bitterly cold weather and swinging wide the hips to mush along on bearpaw snowshoes will prey on any weak spots in your skeletal system. That night I spent fifteen hours in a soft bed in a frigid cabin while the dogs shivered in their sleep on the floor. The next morning I could barely move, and the thought of driving home a thousand miles on horrendous roads in a lurching motorhome was almost as unbearable as actually doing it.

I pulled into my driveway on December 18. A call to the contact in International Falls brought news both depressing and delightful. "It's 28 below now," he said. "It's going to 40 below tonight and the wind is supposed to increase tomorrow. It wouldn't be very smart to drive out of town 50 miles to go spruce grouse hunting."

Top: The spruce grouse is well distributed throughout the continent's northern boreal coniferous forest. Note the bit of red above the eye of this male, photographed in fall. (Photograph - Tom Huggler))
Bottom: This young spruce grouse is tensed to fly. Because of their lack of fear, the spruce is the least sporting of the grouse to hunt. Hunting pressure, however, teaches the bird that man is just another predator. (Photograph - Tom Huggler)

Relieved to be off the hook, I agreed but was still disappointed. I knew I had made the right decision, though, when the phone rang an hour later. It was Brian Kadrmas, the young taxidermist from Bismarck who is mounting all the species of North American grouse for me.

"I've got a fine specimen of a male spruce grouse that I shot in Alaska last fall," he said. "It's yours if you want it."

I wanted it.

There will be other times and places to hunt spruce grouse, if not with a dog and gun, then with a camera. Leopold put it in proper perspective when he wrote: "A man may not care for golf and still be human, but the man who does not like to see, hunt, photograph or otherwise outwit birds or animals is hardly normal."

It is nice to be normal.

Many hunters take advantage of the spruce grouse's lack of fear and need for grit by hunting along roads.
(Photograph - Tom Huggler)

"What else was there to know about ruffed grouse? Gardiner Bump had done it all, or so I thought."

—**Gordon Gullion**

The Grouse Researchers

Cloquet Forestry Center. October 2, 1989:

On the drive north to the entrance off Minnesota Highway 210 East, you will notice the checkerboard cuttings in the aspens. The aspens are his and the grouse's favorite tree. The office itself is a small log cabin nestled among wind-tossed pines—that other tree. You will know which cabin is his by the red Ford Ranger with the white top and the Ruffed Grouse Society beige sticker on the rear window. The vanity license plate says "Bonasa."

Cloquet Forestry Center, operated by the University of Minnesota, dates from 1909. Among American university forestry departments, only Yale is older. The building and his office are old. The light switch is the push-button type, and you suspect behind the walls lies knob-and-tube wiring. The file cabinets are a Depression-era green. The carpet needs replacing. Along one wall an ancient desk of heavy oak supports a Royal manual typewriter with green keys. Papers also roost on the desk, to a depth of several inches.

Along the other wall, a wooden door spans a pair of low file cabinets. This makeshift desk is also piled high with literature.

On the walls, maps shaded with colored pencils hold red and yellow stickpins. The pins represent ruffed grouse sightings, both at the Cloquet Forest and Mille Lacs Research Center, which is ninety miles away. A sign on another wall says, "You may smoke but please don't exhale." Somewhere in the mountain of paperwork, the telephone rings, and Gordon Gullion excuses himself to answer it. Outside, autumn presses against the windowpane with leaves of red, yellow and orange. Chickadees, phoebes and a red squirrel jockey for space at the bird feeder.

This grouse is about to fly from a fall drumming log. Grouse males of all species visit leks and drumming grounds in fall, although the display periods are to establish territories and learn techniques–not to attract hens.
(Photograph - Richard P. Smith)

This is the setting where Gordon Gullion, the world's number one ruffed grouse researcher, has worked since 1958, and where he will retire exactly one year from this interview day. Born and raised in Eugene, Oregon, Gullion attended the University of Oregon and earned his masters degree from the University of California at Berkley. There, he was the student of Starker Leopold, Aldo's son. Gullion spent a few years working with valley quail and sage grouse in Nevada, then came east for a change of climate and job. "I had no attraction to ruffed grouse per se," he said. "The job came up and I wanted to leave administrative work and get back into research."

The purpose of research at the Cloquet Forestry Center was and is to see how forestry management practices can best benefit ruffed grouse. Gullion thought he would be reworking Ralph King's old data, gathered at Cloquet during the period 1931-36. King was a contemporary of Gardiner Bump, who headed the New York investigation that resulted in the exhaustive 900-page work, *The Ruffed Grouse: Life History, Propogation, Management* published in 1947.

"What else was there to know about ruffed grouse?" Gullion said. "Gardiner Bump had done it all, or so I thought."

A year into his new job, Gullion realized that he needed to understand all aspects of grouse behavior. He was one of the first wildlife researchers to use radio-telemetry and relied heavily on it during the period 1960-65. In the winter of 1963, Gullion concluded that aspen is the basic habitat for ruffed grouse. He wrote that "...it is not a coincidence that the most widely distributed resident gamebird in North America correlates closely with the range of the most widely distributed forest tree on the continent."

This discovery is his significant contribution to the research. Others, of course, had pointed out the relationship of grouse to aspen (Leopold: "Thus to me the aspen is in good repute because he glorifies October and he feeds my grouse in winter"), but no one had asked the question, "Why?" Gordon Gullion has dedicated his life's work to finding the answers.

Some of those answers lie buried in the rows of IBM cards in his bulging file cabinets. A sometime hunter of ruffed grouse, Gullion is also a writer of popular literature on these regal birds. The scientific and sporting communities alike eagerly await his retirement when he will have more time for both pursuits. Perhaps he will write a sequel to his *Grouse of the North Shore*.

The objective researcher draws conclusions from his findings. Over the years as the raw-data evidence mounts, the findings may counter earlier beliefs. Gullion no longer

Top left: Gordon Gullion has spent more than 30 years researching grouse at the Cloquet Forestry Center in Minnesota. (Photograph - Tom Huggler)
Top right: Sharptails are capable of flying long distances. (Photograph - Ron Spomer)
Bottom: Ruffed grouse display between drumming and when threatened by intruders, including other male grouse. (Photograph - Maslowski)

supports irregular checkerboard cutting of timber for two reasons: (1) the cost is too high, (2) birds don't live on the edge—they die there. Raptors use trees along the edge as sentry posts to prey upon drumming cock grouse foolish enough to set up shop there. "Until recently, the size of clearcuts was less important than I thought," Gullion explained.

Another question begging for more research: Do we still need the old forest nearby? Grouse are extremely selective, and, for some reason, they will pick out individual trees that are in physiological difficulty—disadvantaged trees, for example, that grow along slopes or are fire-scarred or decayed. "Perhaps foresters should cut the healthy aspen, which grouse don't target, and leave the poor ones," is a conclusion that Gullion would not have made a few years ago.

More chemical research is needed, but it is expensive. Only aspen that is fourteen years or older produces the flowering buds that grouse love to eat, but during a two- or three-week period each year the scales produce a toxic chemical.

"Why the poisonous production?" Gullion wonders. "Is it a defense against animal predation? The result of solar radiation? We simply don't know."

Recent studies showing that depressed numbers of waterfowl will not pioneer new areas of prime habitat may have significance for ruffed grouse management. "We need to address the impact of hunting on ruffed grouse populations," Gullion believes. "It is more significant than I originally thought." Research in the sandhill country of Wisconsin, for example, shows that maximum hunting pressure is only one-half hunter per hour per acre. Studies at Mille Lacs, which absorbs high hunting pressure, indicate that good habitat does not necessarily draw new grouse to it. Gullion's preliminary conclusion: "There is no automatic replacement to a burned-out breeding area."

In recent years, he has grown concerned that late hunting seasons remove safe breeders, which creates a void in the habitat the following spring. "Much of the literature says that 40 to 45 percent of the grouse population can be harvested each year," he said. "Bump thought the safe figure lay closer to 17 percent. I believe the truth may be somewhere between." A disturbing thought: Studies show that eight of every ten grouse shot after Thanksgiving would have been breeders the following year.

Many researchers believe that grouse will adapt to a given habitat. Gullion disagrees. "My feeling is that grouse are not very adaptable at all," he said. "They are limited, and so they utilize habitats that are similar." Uncut aspen forests in Minnesota produced only .7

Ruffed grouse often gather in the winter to roost and feed. These five birds were photographed while budding. (Photograph - Richard P. Smith)

drumming males per 100 acres, compared to 15.5 drummers for those areas aggressively managed. Intensive aspen management in Vermont has resulted in a 200 to 300 percent increase in grouse.

Gullion's position is that grouse do better without conifers, but he acknowledges the disagreement of several colleagues. A current study in the Happy Valley Area Project near Syracuse, New York, may provide answers. In Tennesee and Missouri, researchers want to know if ruffed grouse will adapt to oak-hickory forests.

The more we learn about grouse, the more we need to know. Are red-phase grouse more aggressive, as Bergerud has written, and do they push out the gray subspecies? What is the longevity of grouse to certain forest types? How do micro-climactic changes impact grouse?

Asked to crystal-ball the future for grouse, Gullion said he is encouraged by the tremendous interest shown in grouse throughout the country, largely due to the Ruffed Grouse Society. The future is especially good in the Great Lakes region, thanks to aggressive forest-cutting practices. As a result, grouse numbers may not decline there in the 1990s and beyond. The future of grouse in the Ohio River Valley depends on the environmentalists and their dogged fight against clear cutting. As a result, grouse habitat in Ohio, Indiana and Illinois is suffering from the lack of cutting. New England, Maine and upstate New Hampshire and Vermont are in good shape, but other areas, namely Massachusetts and Connecticut, are on the tag end of aspen longevity and desperately need cutting.

Private landowners, reluctant to remove their mature trees, need to realize how such stagnation hurts wildlife. Studies in Pennsylvania show that checkerboard cuts as small as two and one half acres can have a positive impact on grouse. White-tailed deer and ruffed grouse usually thrive in young forest habitats. In some areas, though, too many whitetails superimposed on that habitat ruin it for grouse because the deer will overly browse the understory.

The amount of work yet to do makes one wish that Gordon Gullion was beginning, not ending, his career as a scientific investigator.

Guilderland, New York. December 11, 1989:

The southern New York hills along Highway 88 are snow-covered. Powerline clearings in the bare woods look like reverse-Mohawk haircuts. The rivers are frozen this morning, and the temperature has stalled at 32 degrees. The sky is the color of pewter; gray clouds roll away like a rumpled woolen blanket.

Top: Catching a flushing grouse in the open is unusual. (Photograph - Ron Spomer)
Bottom: A ruffed grouse on the wing may be the toughest target to bag among upland species. (Photograph - Maslowski)

"You never know where you will find grouse," Carl Parker says. "They're not always in aspen. They use ironwood, witch hazel and gray dogwood, sometimes in preference to aspen. Opening the crops of seven birds one day, we were surprised to find they had been stuffing themselves with skunk cabbage fruits. Who would have guessed it?"

The joy of discovery. The thrill of learning something new. Those are the mystical drawing cards the ruffed grouse holds for its students—university-trained researcher and woods-wise hunter alike. Carl Parker is a hunter. He retired from the New York Department of Environmental Conservation in 1983 after serving a distinguished career as Fisheries Division Chief. But he would rather hunt ruffed grouse than catch rainbow trout. How to tell?

Taped to Carl's apartment door in Guilderland, a bedroom community of Albany, is the tailfeather of a red-phase bird. Inside his modest dwelling is a library of books and magazine articles containing everything he knows that has been written about ruffed grouse. Grouse art adorns the walls. In a special wooden box lie 125 tail fans, carefully preserved and artfully arranged. The colors are varying shades of rust, cinnamon, mahogany, gray, brown and taupe.

"I used to collect only the perfect ones," Parker explains. "Then I realized the imperfect ones were more interesting. Tails tell good stories. A hawk tore most of these out."

A notebook records details of the 647 grouse Parker has shot, mostly without the aid of a dog (he has never owned one), since 1961. That was the year he began his passionate pursuits. At 66, he continues walking for grouse each fall.

If my math is correct, his 29-year average is about 23 grouse per season. Not bad for a dogless bird hunter.

"Every grouse that flies before the gun enjoys at least three-to-one odds," Parker once wrote in rebuttal to an anti-hunter whose letter to the editor appeared in a local newspaper. "Meanwhile, the hunter enjoys his exercise and recharges his psychic battery as he walks the purple hills. If a bird falls, he shares a gourmet item with his family. If none falls, he remembers the hills, and that is enough."

He also remembers the covers, the weathers, the flushes, the missed shots, and the few times when bird and shot string came together in mid-air. "You have to go grouse hunting when facial tics begin to develop and you feel like beating the cat," Carl philosophized over coffee in his apartment.

Carl Parker of Guilderland, NY, has collected more than 125 grouse fans during a 30-year hunting career. Carl shows two of more than 30 color phases. (Photograph - Tom Huggler)

"To be normal again, all I need is one grouse to flush, and maybe have a chance for a shot."

I drove on into New England, kicking myself for not budgeting time to hunt with Carl Parker. I would have liked to have hunted with several other self-taught researchers, too, if not in the field, then at least in their recollections. Men like H.G. "Tap" Tapply of *Field & Stream* fame. Now 80 years old, Tap hunted for 20 years with Burton Spiller and spent "fifty good years" in grouse woods before ligament surgery on his right knee forced him to case his 20 gauge Winchester Model 21. A blizzard kept me from stopping by his home in East Alton, New Hampshire, to ask what the covers were like in the 30s and 40s, even though I could imagine the answer. Webb B. White, 95, offered to describe to me the Massachusetts covers of the 1920s, which he hunted after moving to the Bay State from Iowa. Bedridden at his home in Weston, Massachusetts, he was unable, sadly, to receive visitors.

I could have spent hours, days actually, talking to such men and to the other researchers—those biologists and scientists who have dedicated their lives to the pursuit of grouse knowledge. Men like Paul Johnsgard of the University of Nebraska who has authored some 17 books, including several on gamebirds. Or Clait Braun, who has compiled more than 20 years of research on white-tailed ptarmigan in Colorado. Or the husband-wife team of Fred and Fran Hamerstrom, students of Aldo Leopold. The Hamerstroms worked with prairie chickens for more than a half-century and were responsible for their successful reintroduction in Wisconsin.

It is easy to become fascinated with grouse. And hunting grouse adds an exciting dimension to inquiry.

A hunt in the bench and coulee country of north central Montana produced these sharptails. (Photograph - Tom Huggler)

"I had no choice but to travel alone, because I was taking notes and stopping everywhere to write them. I could think clearly only when I was alone, and then my imagination began to work as my mind wandered."

—**Paul Theroux**

Epilogue

The more we travel, the farther from home we have to go. Hunting grouse was the pretext for going, but any hunter knows that much more is involved than dead bird weight in a gamebag. What follows are a few of the things I'll long remember from my travels for grouse.

The Other Migrants

As I drove the continent back and forth, I cut across the travel routes of other migrants. In early September, monarch butterflies drifted south over the Iowa interstate on their way to Central America. On a journey more fraught with danger than mine, some of them missed the motorhome grille and briefly flared orange as they washed up and over the windshield to safety.

In North Dakota, crane skeins pinwheeled under a gray vault of clouds. Closer to earth, the snow geese, their black-tipped white wings undulating like a spectators' wave in a football stadium, rode a tail wind from the northwest. Closer still, horned larks and buntings, two of the arctic's most prolific visitors, flashed white in little bursts of speed along the road shoulder.

Later, while hunting among hills of little bluestem near Medina, we saw hundreds of cliff swallows rising and falling before a wind that tearstreaked our faces. One swallow, missing a primary or two on the left wing, worked overtime. I wondered how many extra wingbeats she had made on what must have seemed an interminable flight down from Baker Lake in the Northwest Territories. How many more wingpumps before Guatemala could be realized? Fluidity and grace are all, or so the birds would teach us.

There were east/west migrants, too. The concrete road opens and swallows, allowing passage for all transients at 65 miles per hour. Two new black tractor trucks piggy-backed to the fifth wheel of a third rig looked like rutting Angus bulls. A more sobering

The author stuffs a New England grouse into the gamebag as Tim Leary's setter, Spiller, watches. (Photograph - Tim Leary)

thought was this highway sign in Nebraska: "Please drive carefully. Unmarked nuclear warheads travel these roads."

The semi-truck wheel ruts that bucked the motorhome on I-35 in Kansas made me think of the wagon ruts that lurched the prairie schooners a hundred years ago at Independence Rock in Wyoming. We were both westering. The difference was that at a mile a minute the diesel long-haulers roaring by had a push-pull effect on the motorhome. They rolled air in an invisible wake that shoved me aside and then tried to suck me back to their lane the instant they broke clear.

There is poetry on the open road: Stonehocker Moving and Storage. Leprino Line. The Freymillers dueled with the Freightliners which dueled with the Fruehaufs and the Roadways and the no-neck J. B. Hunt trucks. And the moving vans: low-slung, boxey North American rigs of red, white and blue. The huge orange Stevens outfits and the green-and-yellow Mayflower vans. A fleet of midnight blue-and-silver Steelcase trucks fresh out of Grand Rapids, Michigan, weaved through the jammed Chicago corridor like a pack of thuggish sharks.

In Canada, the company names changed to Laidlaw and Triple Crown Carriers and Thompson Transport. The stainless steel tankers looked like giant thermos bottles on wheels.

There is a cadence and a symmetry to such scenes if you care to listen and to look for it. The rhythmical click of highway expansion joints keeps tune to the steady sway of the motorhome and the squeak of a door ajar. With certain regularity, too, are the passing hills of soft brown and the fitted crop fields that snap into place like a finished puzzle.

The Hunters

Although I had to travel alone, I had to have other people to meet, to hunt with, to photograph, to interview. Some of them showed me their best hunting spots. I used their freezers to keep my grouse specimens from spoiling. I sent near-deadline stories to impatient editors on my friends' word-processing modems. I borrowed their showers and telephones and washing machines and spare bedrooms. My quest became their quest as they became caught up in my adventures.

You and your wife were attending evening classes at the community college when I pulled into the driveway of your Durham, Kansas, home after dark. You had left the door unlocked. "Ham and beans are in the crockpot," the note said, "along with warm cornbread,

Top left: Sharptails often frequent grain fields in the late season, especially when grasshoppers are no longer available. These hunters scored from a wheat stubble field. (Photograph - Dave Books) Top right: Long seasons in many states allow hunting under all weather conditions. This late season hunter used snowshoes to mush to grouse habitat. (Photograph - Tim Leary) Bottom: Thayne Smith and Bill Harmon look over a chicken that Thayne bagged near Harmon's Durham, KS, home. (Photograph - Tom Huggler)

scalloped potatoes and cherry cobbler on the stove. Beer in the fridge. Whiskey in the cabinet. Make yourself to home."

That night, trains roared in the rural darkness and shook the windows in the upstairs bedroom window, just as they had done thirty years ago in another place when I was a kid. I slept so well.

You closed your sporting goods store in West Vail one day to introduce another friend and me to Colorado blue and sage grouse. You, too, love grouse and are the only person I know to have shot an auerhuhn, the world's largest grouse, in Germany, where the lifetime limit is one bird. You moved to Colorado from Wisconsin in 1962 before "condominium" became a household word. We hunted your favorite spot in Eagle County, a place where we watched surveyors map 40-acre homesites. They would sell for $120,000 each. "Enjoy the view," you said bitterly. "This is the last season I'll be able to hunt here."

You were all ages. In Kansas, both of you had retired, ostensibly to add more experiences to the 50 years you had already spent afield in each other's company. Your guns were deadly Browning semi-automatics, and the triggers were shiny. One was a Christmas present from your dad in 1959. That was the year he had given you and your three brothers new guns, then died of a heart attack the next day. You told good Dust Bowl stories and talked freely about a hunting accident in 1947, not long after you had returned from the war. A loaded 16-gauge Long Tom with 36-inch barrel and a faulty firing pin. The car door handle hit the gun's hammer, which, oddly, was not cocked. But the gun discharged anyway, and you nearly lost your foot. The doctors didn't want to cut off your new cowboy boots, but you told them to do it and then joked about the prospect of getting another purple heart.

Sometimes you were thirteen, all mouth braces and long legs that wound up somewhere around your ears. You carried your grandfather's 20-gauge 870 pumpgun as though it was a carton of eggs. I carried the sharp-tailed grouse you shot because you had forgotten to slip on a hunting vest over the Batman tee shirt you wore.

And you were an eighteen-year-old daughter, a college freshman majoring in business management in Bismarck. You shot your mother's 20-gauge pump, a gun she had won at the Ducks Unlimited banquet. You had on her sweater, too, along with your own Reeboks and jeans. You and your golden retrievers, Casey and her four-month-old daughter, Trouble, led us to the sharptails and the Hungarian partridge. You said birds were easy, having shot a whitetail buck every year of your young hunting life.

Top: College student Kelly Jo Holtan hunts sharptails in North Dakota with her golden retriever. (Photograph - Tom Huggler)
Bottom: The author (right) discusses hunting strategy with Jerry Dennis (left) and Tom Carney while ruffed grouse hunting in the upper peninsula of Michigan. (Photograph - Randy Carrels)

The Dogs

I enjoyed them all. In Nebraska, you loaded the veteran Schultz and 12-month-old Trina, both shorthairs, into my trailer. "I wish I could take the other 31 I have to leave behind," you said. The two shorthairs joined my Labrador and Brittany, then later we added your cousins' dogs—Gertie and Bart (more shorthairs) and Rowdy, another Brittany. Seven dogs in all. Were we hunting grouse or black bear?

Trina showed incredible courage after biting a porcupine in Colorado. We muzzled her with a handkerchief, and two of us held her down while you painfully removed the quills with the edge of your knife blade. The indignant little shorthair ran off to go hunting. An hour later, she pointed her first sage grouse.

In Wyoming, my Brittany finally learned that he could not catch a pronghorn. I laughed at this, remembering how a few days earlier I had lost him in a Colorado mountain pass and worried myself sick for five minutes, certain he had chased a marmot off a cliff. So we laughed at Reggie and also at happy little Tillie, your U-shaped setter, who grinned while swatting her nose with her tail, left and right, left and right.

In Montana, we swam our dogs in the coolness of stock watering tanks. Your viszla shook himself dry, his stub tail twitching like an overactive paint brush. The otter-like tail of my Labrador whipped left and right like a windshield wiper. Fresh from the tank, she made her hose of a tail to throw figure eights of water for up to ten feet.

Each dog was special. In Montana, your two-year-old golden, Tanker, held a blue grouse for the camera until his jaws ached. Mysti, another golden, did the same with a lesser prairie chicken in Kansas. In Michigan, Coach, your young golden, learned to love grouse as much as our unattended raw omelette mix. In Vermont, Spiller had the name, blood lines, looks and hunting abilities that a man expects from a classic New England setter.

The Land Forms and Weathers

Barry Lopez wrote, "One learns a landscape not by knowing the name or identity of everything in it, but by perceiving the relationships in it."

Walking through landscape is the best way to perceive those relationships. It wasn't necessary to wear a pedometer to realize I tramped a few hundred miles. Looking for sharptails on the High Plains of Nebraska brought us to Johnny Foster's homestead on a

Top left: Dogs cover three to five miles for every mile the hunter walks. When sharptails are the target, either hunter can wear out first. (Photograph - Ron Spomer)
Top right: The author admits to a fondness for English setters, although he has hunted grouse behind many other breeds, including his own Brittany and yellow Labrador. (Photograph - Tom Huggler)
Bottom: Reggie, the author's Brittany, retrieves a sharptail. (Photograph - Tom Huggler)

Saturday afternoon in September. A deaf mute, Foster had come out in 1902 from Iowa or Illinois and proved up on the place in 1914. When his wife died, childless, about 1944, Johnny gave up the farm and left for Oregon to live with relatives. Today, he is buried in the local cemetery next to his wife. Trees and brush slowly reclaim the homestead. Inside the crumbling walls, we read penciled notations on a bare cupboard. They chronicled the deaths of Johnny's mother in 1929 and certain friends and favorite animals.

In Nebraska's Sand Hills the lemon-colored moon, looking like a scuffed tennis ball, hung large and low in the western sky. The early morning light was coming now. It illuminated the sand dunes with low-angle intensity, so that they resembled ripples on a sandy lake bottom. Indeed, they say there was a great saltwater lake here millions of years ago, but the buckskin-colored hills and their voluptuous darker folds were formed in another time and way—from wind blowing unchecked across dried river beds. The scene reminded me of northern Spain. Instead of goatherders driving their flocks across some dry saddle, though, the animals in this place were cattle with red and green tags in their ears. And the drovers were mounted cowboys.

More landscapes. In eastern Montana, much of the land remains untamed. There are places here that are 100 miles from gasoline stations. One-third to one-half of the state's counties, some of which are the size of Masachusetts, contain no traffic lights. Children are bused so far to public schools that they must stay in dormitories until the weekend.

Montana Highway 200 twists and turns its gray way east for hundreds of miles through country that alternates between badlands and rangelands. Buttes and ravines are cut by erosion, which has exposed seams of bedrock. The predominate colors are dusty tan, parched gray, and here and there a streak of magenta from some type of ground covering. Mule deer country. No homes. No farms. One of the few regions in America where I was unable to get anything on the radio.

Portions of Wyoming are equally desolate. On Highway 487 at the entrance to the Shirley Basin, I waited for a half-dozen 637D Caterpillar earthmovers to pass in single file before I could drive forward. They looked like giant yellow dinosaurs chasing each other, which made me think of the rich finds of dinosaur bones the region has served up during the past century. Wyoming must have been wet then, possibly covered by a brackish sea, and certainly there was abundant plant life to feed the mostly vegetarian beasts. Today, the land is so dry the road builders must pump in water to soak the earth in order to scrape it for new pavement.

Top: Sage grouse distribution is keyed to sagebrush. After a population low in the 1930s and 40s,
the birds have made a comeback in some areas. (Photograph - Ron Spomer)
Bottom: Ruffed grouse are particularly adapted to northern forested areas. Although the birds themselves are not always visible,
evidence of their existence is often indicated by flush marks in the snow. (Photograph - Tom Klein)

Much of North America lay locked in drought during my travels. The western mountains had collected little snowpack in recent winters, and rainfall had been in short supply for as long as three years. In Minnesota, a huge field of dried sunflowers, heads hanging to the east, looked like thousands of Moslems at prayer. In North Dakota, the potholes, normally full of water in fall, resembled dirty sponges that had dried. In Wyoming, 30 minutes after I had emptied out a thermos of cold coffee into the ground, I could not find the spot.

The farther west one travels, the shorter in height are the plant forms. A dearth of water is the reason. Corn, for example, is shorter in Nebraska than in Iowa, and wheat is likewise shorter in eastern Colorado than in Nebraska or Kansas. This phenomenon was also true of the original plant forms. The tallgrass prairie that sprang up in the Midwest extended to eastern Kansas, then changed to shortgrass varieties in the western part of the state.

The dryness of the West made me appreciate chapstick, talcum powder and hand lotion. The wetness of the Midwest made me glad for a waterproof Grouse Parka by Columbia Sportswear. The bitter cold of New England for polypropylene and the company's insulated Chukar Parka.

On the Great Plains, the wind skipped tumbleweeds across the highway to startle me. Wind sculps clouds in strange ways. Some were cantilevered, smooth-bottom formations with puffy heads. Other, pregnant with rain, wore dark veins and some had their bottoms torn away. A few had a feathered look that could be deceiving. What I thought were clouds atop Mt. Washington in New Hampshire were actually plumes of snow driven by 100 mile-an-hour winds.

The weathers were a mixed bag—from 97 degree heat in Montana to 20 degrees below zero in New England. It snowed in Colorado and in Michigan and in New Hampshire. When it wasn't snowing in Michigan, it rained, and that was all right, too.

Hunters earn a satisfaction when they have beaten the elements. I thought about that while drying off in a truck with two friends after hunting in a Michigan rainstorm for ruffed grouse. We shared a can of Old Style beer and listened to the rain drum on the pickup cab. The truck was warm. Looking out the side window, I noticed that a carpet of wet maple leaves has a certain brilliance that occurs only on days when the sky is the color of iron. Tops of the leaves are a blood-red; underneath, the lovely pink undersides are lightly veined with scarlet.

I don't remember if we shot any grouse that day.

Top left: A blue-grouse hunter climbs a grassy ridge beside conifer forest — note the edge habitat. (Photograph - Ron Spomer)
Top right: The author hunted with Ron Spomer in Wyoming and Kansas. (Photograph - Tom Huggler)
Bottom: Sharptails are the second most popular grouse in North America. Grasslands are a key to their survival —
this scene was photographed in Waterton National Park. (Photograph - Michael Francis) On following pages: October is the
grouse hunter's month. This scene was photographed in Vermont. (Photograph - Tim Leary)